The SHED Method

The SHED Method

Making Better Choices Easier

The SHED Method

Making Better Choices When it Matters

SARA MILNE ROWE

MICHAEL JOSEPH
an imprint of
PENGUIN BOOKS

MICHAEL JOSEPH

UK | USA | Canada | Ireland | Australia
India | New Zealand | South Africa

Michael Joseph is part of the Penguin Random House group of companies
whose addresses can be found at global.penguinrandomhouse.com.

First published by Michael Joseph
001

Text copyright © Sara Milne Rowe, 2018
Illustrations by Simon Pearsall

The moral right of the authors and illustrator has been asserted

All names have been changed except in a few instances where clients
have granted permission for their stories to be shared.

Set in 13/15.43 pt Garamond MT Std
Typeset by Jouve (UK), Milton Keynes
Printed in Great Britain by Clays Ltd, St Ives plc

A CIP catalogue record for this book is available from the British Library

ISBN: 978—0—718—18395—0

www.greenpenguin.co.uk

Penguin Random House is committed to a
sustainable future for our business, our readers
and our planet. This book is made from Forest
Stewardship Council® certified paper.

To my mother, Vita, and to my business partner, Simon,
without whom this book would never have emerged.

I believe that we learn by practice. Whether it means to learn to dance by practising dancing or to learn to live by practising living, the principles are the same. In each, it is the performance of a dedicated precise set of acts, physical or intellectual, from which comes shape of achievement, a sense of one's being, a satisfaction of spirit.

Martha Graham

Contents

Contents

Better Choices

I.

Wishing to be better at something lies at the heart of most of the conversations I have with people. What they mean by better is always different. For me, *better* is energy-giving, flourishing, stretching, thriving, making progress one step at a time. *Better* is healing. *Better* is about believing you can be – and do – more than you thought. And at the heart of becoming better at anything is the ability to make better choices. That's what I help people to do.

When I meet any client, step one is finding out what specifically they wish to be better at – and it's not always straightforward. As we work together and discuss their situation, their strengths, their hopes and ambitions – they often realize that what they actually want to be better at is not what they were thinking when they walked in. Here's an example close to my heart:

Back in 2000, after having had both my children, I chose to move on from my full-time job as a teacher in an inner-city comprehensive to set up my own business – in performance coaching. It seemed to make perfect sense. A natural segue from helping, nudging and challenging teenagers from all cultures to focus and do their best, to helping, nudging and challenging people from all backgrounds to have more impact, to be more confident and more successful – whatever that meant to them. Taking that leap of faith was a risk. And there were many times in those early days when the responsibility of building a business left me feeling uncomfortably challenged, overwhelmed and frankly just not good enough. No one in my family had ever started a business, and I needed to be better at understanding how to build one. Or so I thought. After months of frustration I finally worked out that, in order to do that, first of all I needed to be a lot better at managing myself in those moments when feeling 'not good enough' hit me. I made a commitment to do just that: to be better at being my own judge; to allow myself to choose when and if I was good enough and what I needed to do to be just that.

I knew that learning to manage this feeling would take effort and practice but, if I could crack it, it would definitely be worth it. I began to pay more attention to those moments when it surfaced. I became a scientist around my own feelings and behaviour, and started to keep a record:

- When did the feeling occur?

- What prompted it?

- What did my body do?

- What did I start to think?

- What was the impact?

Continuing to fall victim to these old feelings wasn't my idea of fun, but at least it meant I had plenty of data to analyse, experiment with and learn from. I noticed some patterns around my reactions and what prompted them. Now I had this bulk of evidence, the question was, how do I interrupt those feelings, lessen their impact and enable myself to perform at my best?

I make no apology for using the word *perform*, by the way. It is a huge part of my background and, I believe, lies at the heart of becoming better . . . at anything. When clients say, 'I don't want to perform and pretend to be someone I'm not,' I will often ask, 'How do you know you'd be someone you're not? What if you discovered you could be more than you are?'

One of my favourite quotes is: 'We can act our way into a new way of thinking as well as think our way into a new way of acting.' By acting or performing our way into a new way of thinking, we can sometimes unearth elements of us that we didn't believe were possible.

That's what I had to do. I needed to find some practical ways to perform better: to manage myself and become more resilient so I could create the business I wanted. I started to consider those situations in my past when I had worked to be better at something – becoming a better dancer as a child, a better violinist as a teenager, a better teacher as an adult. I decided to extract the key ingredients that made up being a better performer in each of those situations, and build them into useful practices. As I examined them more closely and experimented with the outcomes – first by myself, then working with family, friends and clients – I gradually developed a set of core practices. Finally, I had a toolkit that I could call on to choose a better set of responses and take back control.

I now help people all over the world to develop their own simple and practical ways to achieve what they want: whether that's to be better at communicating with their child, leading their team, managing themselves under increasing pressure, reaching a goal, or even setting up their own business. As their coach I work with them to define clearly that certain something they need to be better at, and to apply the practices that will help them achieve it.

I never intended to write a book. I was cajoled by clients who said things like:

- Why isn't this stuff in a book? It's made everything a lot clearer and I want a reminder.

- People have noticed a change in how I'm reacting to things that used to drive me mad and ask me what I mean when I say, 'I'm choosing my mood.'

- If this was in a book I could keep it on my desk to refer to every time I feel nervous.

• I'm surprised by how choosing to shift my
morning routine in such a small way could have
such an impact on my ability to focus. Everyone
should know this.

So here it is.

A practical, useful book – a human manual – to help
you make better choices so you can do and be better when
it really matters. A book to pick up whenever you think
you need it, whoever you are, whatever you're doing, be it
dealing with a difficult conversation, coping with anxious
children, facing challenges at work or managing yourself
when you're up against it.

In this book I describe the method I use with clients:
the SHED method. It includes a series of practices, personal routines and rituals that have evolved from thousands
of hours' coaching hundreds of people, from CEOs to
students, from professionals to parents – practices and
routines that have helped them to make better choices,
whether for themselves, for colleagues or for family and
friends, and which can do the same for you. The tools
and techniques in this method are derived from personal
performance experience, are supported by science, and
echo the habits of high performers who've built tried
and tested ways to remain at their best – often achieving
more than they thought possible. If you follow this
method, arming yourself with a bespoke series of practices and clear steps, you too will be able to make better
choices in the moments that matter to you and to those
around you.

Crucially, to be better for others, the work *has* to start with you. It's much harder to be better for others when you yourself are feeling exhausted, out of control, frustrated or 'not good enough'. To be better for others, you need to know how to choose to get the best from yourself. That is the aim of this book. Just as other manuals help you get the best out of your washing machine, vacuum cleaner or boiler, this book can help get the best out of you. And, like any other manual, it has a troubleshooting section at the back, with handy tips to dip into when you want to find a quick and simple answer.

START WITH YOU

If you were sitting in front of me now, I would ask you, 'What do you want to be better at?'

If the word *better* feels scary to you, you're not alone. For some, it can feel energy-sapping rather than energy-giving – a million miles from flourishing or thriving. For many it smacks of old school reports ('could do better') or brings up negative and unhelpful comparisons ('they do it better than me'). For some, the concept of becoming better at anything demands a level of self-belief or awareness that they perhaps feel they lack, or a level of determination, grit or self-preservation that sounds exhausting when they feel strung out as it is. If you are one of those people, I invite you to step forward and answer this question: How much better dare you be?

In answer to that question, many people I meet start by describing their current reality. For example:

_____ Things are tough at the moment.

_____ I need to make some decisions.

_____ My team/son/daughter is anxious.

_____ There is so much going on and I am overstretched.

_____ I have three months to sort this out.

_____ X is driving me mad.

_____ I seem to always be in meetings.

_____ I feel bored and underchallenged.

As far as they are concerned, for them to become better, someone or something else has to change first:

- If he would just listen more . . .
- If they were to ask me what I thought . . .
- If she would only stop . . .
- If I had more time . . .
- If they got home earlier . . .
- If I could do more work from home . . .
- If they would just get on with it . . .
- If the place wasn't so . . .
- If they would just make a decision . . .

9

However, when they start to connect instead with what *they* can do – with what *they* can control – I witness a shift in their motivation to choose to do something different. Once I sense this, we return to the question: 'What do *you* want to be better at?'

Here are some common responses:

- Better at listening.
- Better at managing my emotions.
- Better at saying no.
- Better at switching off.
- Better at going to bed earlier.
- Better at spending time with friends/my family.
- Better at making decisions.
- Better at being positive.
- Better at speaking out.
- Better at saying what I want.
- Better at looking and feeling confident.
- Better at concentrating.
- Better at prioritizing.
- Better at asking questions.
- Better at influencing.

Once people can begin to articulate something specific that they can do, take responsibility for and control, a sense of choice begins to take root, and they move from being a spectator to a participant.

My aim is then to help them build their desire to achieve their ambition by asking more questions:

- Why is this important to you?

- When have you done this well in the past?

- How did you know?

- What would being better at it feel like? Look like? Sound like?

- Who would benefit?

- In what situation(s) do you want to be better at it?

- How will you know that being better at it was worth it?

- And finally, how would you currently rate your ability at doing it on a scale of 1 to 10 (where 1 = very poor and 10 = excellent)?

This last question is important, as it helps clients to mark where they are when they set off, and offers them a simple way of measuring progress as they continue on their journey.

Of course you might already be very good at what you want to be better at, so, for you, better means becoming exceptional. Many people I work with find it hugely energizing to keep learning to be even better.

Recently I was working with a client on a keynote speech to his entire company. He performed really well and the audience feedback was excellent – the average score his speech received was 8.1 out of 10. I sent him the footage. Within an hour he had downloaded it, watched it and sent me a return email saying, 'Thanks for this. I'm happy with the audience reaction and how I came across. Personally, I would rate my performance at around 7. I'm telling you now that by my next presentation I want to be scoring 9.' Some people would be happy with an audience rating of 8.1. But, for him, being better meant pushing himself even closer to 10.

So, here's the question. Where do you want *better* to take you?

This book will help you on your journey, sharing examples of how others have gone from:

- lethargy to energy
- furious to curious
- disconnected to connected
- indifferent to driven
- overwhelmed to over it

You choose what *better* means to you. Decide what you want to go from and what you want to become.

One reason the concept of becoming better can scare us is that it requires us to step out of a place that we recognize and have possibly grown comfortable with. Something that describes us. A label. A few of the most frequent labels I see or hear are:

- I'm not good with change.

- I say it how it is.

- I'm risk-averse.

- I'm not really a people person.

- I'm shy.

- I'm loud.

- I'm moody.

- I'm a joker.

- I'm not creative.

- I'm sensitive.

- I tend to overreact.

- I'm not very resilient.

- I don't do 'vulnerable'.

- I'm bloody great.

I regularly meet people who carry this kind of label, either one that they've chosen for themselves or have been given by others. They wear it believing it is who they are. It limits them. It doesn't have to.

That's not to say, of course, that all labels are limiting. Quite often the people who come to me are anxious because they have been given a positive label by someone else and fear they can't live up to it. They ask me to help them test that assumption. What would it take to believe and accept that label and maximize it? What else might be possible?

Over the years I've witnessed students and many clients who felt they couldn't do something because it wasn't them. So they didn't try. I've also met many who were courageous enough to have a go, realize they can do it, and flourish once they discover that they can be more than they thought. Having a fixed sense of who we are can hold us back when we want to up our game and be better at something. I regularly witness people who have trapped themselves into a way of thinking that limits their journey before they've even embarked on it. Old patterns of thought and action can box us in. They give us a limiting sense of who we can be. When we're brave enough to try something else – to have a go and learn from the experience – we can often change what we understand to be possible or worth doing, and ultimately who we believe ourselves to be.

One label that hits us all at some point – from those around us, from ourselves, from society – is the label 'too old'. In 1979, a scientific research project run by Professor Ellen Langer, a Harvard psychologist, looked to prove what was possible when a group of old people were encouraged to step away from that label. The results were extraordinary.

My mother used to say, 'Old age has nothing to

recommend it.' And when Professor Langer announced that she was looking for elderly men in their seventies and eighties for what she described as a 'week of reminiscence', it was no surprise that the group was pretty soon full with volunteers.

What she didn't tell them was that they would unknowingly be taking part in a study of ageing – an experiment that would drop them right back to 1959, to the world they had inhabited twenty years earlier. Langer was interested in the connection between the mind and the body. If she rewound their minds twenty years, what kind of changes – if any – would the body show?

No surprise that, as the elderly gentlemen were coming forward, Langer felt pangs of concern. 'You have to understand, when these people came to see if they could be in the study and they were walking down the hall to get to my office, they looked like they were on their last legs, so much so that I said to my students, "Why are we doing this? It's too risky."' However, the experiment continued and the men were split into two groups and transported to a retreat outside Boston, Massachusetts, for a week.

The first group would be reminiscing in the traditional sense: discussing what they used to do back in the 1950s and remembering what life had been like.

The second group would be reminiscing in an experimental way. They were placed in a time warp and were asked to act as if it were *actually* 1959. They watched films released at that time, listened to music from that period and discussed events such as NASA's satellite launch that year and Castro's seizing control in Havana, all – and this is the important factor – in the present tense.

Professor Langer hoped that, by placing them in an environment connected with their past and their younger lives, she could help their minds reconnect with their younger, more able selves. She made sure there was nothing that could remind them of their actual age. When they arrived, she didn't help them with their bags. 'I told them they could move them an inch at a time. They could unpack them right at the bus and take up a shirt at a time if that helped.' Once they got inside the retreat, there were no rails on the walls, no gadgets to help old people. The same men who had been 'on their last legs' were now totally immersed in a time when they were twenty years younger.

The men spent a week not being treated as incompetent or sick, and pretty soon Langer could tell it was having an effect. She noted that they were walking faster. Their confidence had improved. They were making their own decisions and even making their own meals.

By the last day, one man had even decided he didn't need his walking stick. And while they waited for the bus to arrive and take them back home, she asked if one of them wanted to play a game of tag. By the time the bus arrived, the old men were in the middle of a spontaneous game of touch football!

The experiment had returned the men to 1959 and they certainly felt much younger mentally, breaking the shackles of the 'too old' label. But what about physically?

Professor Langer took physiological measurements before and after the week's experiment, and the results were stunning. The old men's gait, dexterity, speed of movement, cognitive abilities and memory all measurably improved, while their arthritis lessened and their blood pressure dropped; astonishingly, even their eyesight and hearing got better. Both 'reminiscence' groups showed improvements, but the group who had lived as if it were twenty years earlier improved the most. By encouraging the men to think younger, their bodies followed and actually behaved as if they *were* younger.

In my opinion, this is a powerful example of what can happen to the mind and body when people break away from a limiting label. In this book, I'm inviting you to break away from any limiting labels you might have acquired, to leave them behind you and choose a useful first step to move forward. To train your mind and body to help you define the label you want, and live up to it.

Being better requires certain skills, and if you wanted to be better at a sport, a musical instrument or a language, you would want to learn from the best. You would also want someone on hand to guide you, observe you, push you to get better and help measure your progress. Someone to give you honest feedback and help you reach your ambition — be it winning a medal, reaching grade 8 or becoming fluent.

Learning to walk, as a baby, is a great example of how we acquire a skill. We learn from parents, siblings and peers — those who know how to do it. We stand up, we fall down, we try again and again until we get better at it. We are cheered when we succeed, we are encouraged when it's difficult, we are set challenges to walk a bit further until, eventually, we can do it without thinking.

There isn't an athlete, musician or performer I know of who doesn't deliberately practise to improve too. They have a coach to help them work out the key skills they need to practise. The same is true if you wish to be emotionally better – better at managing you.

This book offers simple ideas, tools and techniques to help you choose the way you want to be, rather than letting your habits decide for you. See it as your portable performance coach, helping you work out how to prepare yourself, manage yourself and stretch yourself.

So, standing in a space free of any limiting labels, with a clearer sense (hopefully!) of where you want to get to, I want to ask you the key question again:

- What do you want to be better at?

If you're still finding it tricky to answer – which many people do, by the way – try this:

- Think of a personal achievement. One you feel particularly proud of. Remember your strengths in that achievement and connect to them.

Now . . .

- Jump forward to a year in the future when you are so much better . . .

- What does being better look like?

- What does being better sound like?

- What does being better feel like?

Write those thoughts down if it helps.

When I ask people to think of something they have already achieved – to connect with their strengths – and from there jump into what the future could be like when they are better, they immediately appear more hopeful and confident, and want to go after it. Revisiting strengths you already have and building on them is a powerful way to develop and grow. In my experience, we all have a lot of them if we really look for them.

So, let's continue:

- Why does being better matter to you? To others?

- When are you currently at your best?

- In what situations do you feel you want to be better?

- What gives you energy?

- What would be at risk if you chose to do nothing?

Finally, make a note of how you would rate yourself on this 'Be Better Scale':

I know what success looks like

0 (not at all) ———————————————— 10 (absolutely)

This really matters to me

0 (not at all) ———————————————— 10 (absolutely)

I know the skill I need to be better at

0 (not at all) ———————————————— 10 (absolutely)

I have a way of practising it when I need to

0 (not at all) ———————————————— 10 (absolutely)

I have a way of checking my progress

0 (not at all) ———————————————— 10 (absolutely)

I have others to let me know how I'm doing

0 (not at all) ———————————————— 10 (absolutely)

I make sure I have fun, chill out and switch off

0 (not at all) ———————————————— 10 (absolutely)

I give myself time to reflect on how I'm doing

0 (not at all) ———————————————— 10 (absolutely)

I notice when I am getting better and treat myself

0 (not at all) ———————————————— 10 (absolutely)

Great. Now that you have a sense of where you are starting from, we can head out on your journey to be better. And remember. Getting better can be easier than we think.

A Way of Thinking About Your Brain

2.

Rachel knew she was prepared for the meeting and how tricky it would be. She led a team who were instrumental in delivering the programme behind a huge structural change to the organization. They'd all worked flat-out for over eighteen months to achieve a change that was going to be phased in over three years. She knew her team were exhausted but fully committed to hitting the deadline. She also knew they were dealing with a lot of increasingly frustrated people within the company. This meeting would give Rachel an opportunity to represent her team and also hear more from those people who would be most affected by the change.

Her boss had set the meeting up. In advance, she and Rachel had agreed that the best approach to such a tricky situation would be to remain open-minded, listen well and digest any key requests so they could explore them in more detail together afterwards. They agreed to highlight the areas where the programme was working well. They had thought everything through and she felt ready. She walked in and took her place at the table, gently resting her elbows on the sides of her chair, feeling relaxed and confident as planned.

There was a bit of casual chat, as always, and then her boss opened the meeting: 'So, as we know, we're here to tell Rachel all the issues you're having.'

Rachel immediately felt herself getting hot. Her heart rate quickened and she felt her body brace. She sat up, her resting arms dropping straight down by her side. *That wasn't the approach we planned. What's she doing?* Rachel said to herself. One colleague began to share their frustration and Rachel, rather than doing as planned and listening in a calm, open-minded way, found herself getting defensive and talking over them before they'd even finished. She tried to regain some composure: *Come on, stick to the original plan: keep listening.* Yet she still found herself coming out with things that she'd had no intention of saying. Out tumbled all the kinds of behaviour she so detested in others. She became more agitated in her increasing determination to make her point, to defend her corner, her team. To show these people just how uninformed they were and prove them wrong. She was off . . . and couldn't stop. When others joined in, she interrupted them too. They then interrupted her in return. Nothing was resolved. The Rachel she had planned to be had left her the moment her boss had opened the meeting. She walked away after the meeting feeling furious, let down and totally unsupported.

For Rachel, feeling unsupported was the equivalent of my old feeling of 'not good enough'. It had the capability to derail her. And it clearly did. Rachel had anticipated the trickiness of the meeting. She knew people were frustrated and likely to come with demands. She felt prepared. What she hadn't fully anticipated was her boss's action. As a consequence, she was overtaken by behaviours that she felt she had no control over – despite her intention to handle the meeting better.

This kind of unexpected reaction is something I hear quite regularly. 'I just said things. I knew they weren't helpful but there was nothing I could do. It just happened, I couldn't help myself. My body went into overdrive. Before I knew it, I had said what I thought.' Responses like this are very common among people under pressure. They want to do something different, new or better. The intention is there, then BANG – something else takes over.

So what's going on?

There is an interesting chain at work here. The moment Rachel heard her boss open the meeting in a way she had not expected, she responded physically. Blood rushed to her neck and chest, her heart rate increased and her body stiffened. It was as if she were under attack. In less than a split second, she went from feeling prepared, open and curious to emotionally unsupported, irritated and defensive. One unexpected sentence from her boss and her body spontaneously reacted. She couldn't stop it. This in turn took her into an emotionally charged dialogue with herself – yanking her attention away from the others and on to herself – to protect her position. Two voices in her head were tussling for control: her irritated emotional response (*What's she doing?*) and her rational thought reminding her to stay calm and listen as planned. All her positive intentions to remain open and in 'listening mode' abandoned her instantly. Her emotional response won the fight, and she found herself unable to take part in the meeting as the rational and curious human she had planned to be.

We've all experienced this at some point. One person's comment, look or action knocks our rationality into touch. If we want to regain our rationality and choose not to 'be bossed' by our physical and emotional reactions, we need to pay conscious attention to them, learn to manage them and keep them aligned.

Many of us believe that we, as humans, are primarily logical and rational creatures. If that were true, Rachel's story would be very different. In fact, experience tells us, and now science is giving us proof, that it is the alignment between our three states – Body first, then Mood and *then* Mind – that most helps us to be who we want to be. We don't actually work the way most of us think we do, and I have found two insights fundamental in helping me and others choose to do anything new or better. They are to do with our brain and our energy.

Firstly, the brain.

Before I explain, I must point out to anyone with an 'ology' in The Brain that the way I'm about to describe it is deliberately non-scientific, because clients tell me that this simple way of understanding how our brain works has been a crucial step on their road to making better choices.

The people I work with find it incredibly useful to see the brain not as one but as *three* brains, each with a different role.

THE HUMAN BRAIN

This is the most familiar to all of us because it is in charge of many of the functions we consider to be most human. It is the more considered of the three and has evolved brilliantly to help us thrive as the world has become more complicated. As you read this, you are using your *Human* brain. It is absorbing the collection of letters on this page, analysing the words and their particular relationship to each other within the sentence and understanding the meaning of the sentence as a result. It is extraordinary.

It is responsible for a range of functions that set us apart from all other living creatures: our ability to think logically, to imagine a future clearly, to be creative, to concentrate, problem-solve and to make considered decisions. It spends most of the day hard at work, processing the information that is all around us – at work, at home, in conversation, from the media – making conscious judgements on how best to thrive in whatever situation. Thriving in the twenty-first century is very different from thriving thousands of years ago. Back then we didn't need to decide what to wear, what to eat for breakfast, which emails to respond to, what to pack in our children's school bags and what route to take to avoid the roadworks – all before 9 a.m. Thousands of years ago, life was simpler. The decisions we were making were based on survival. They concerned hunting, keeping warm and procreating. In winter we slept more, and in summer we maximized the daylight. There was a natural order and our choices were based on that.

Now, on a daily basis, we are bombarded with choices which will theoretically enable us to 'thrive': which TV channels we pick, which mode of transport we take, which make of buggy we choose, how we take our coffee, how we consume our music, the news . . . the list goes on. And in a world where we need to continually make more decisions, we are getting worse at making them. The Human brain is only able to handle such vast amounts of potential input by depending on and almost surrendering to impulses – some useful, some significantly less so.

Do you find yourself:

- Answering your emails in bed?
- Checking your phone every five minutes – even in company and at family meals?
- Not going to the gym, even though you want to?
- Leaving yourself no time to make important decisions?
- Starting lots, finishing nothing?
- Getting cross with people you don't mean to be cross with?
- Agreeing to stuff when you really don't want to?
- Bypassing meals?
- Going to bed much later than you intended?
- Using a mobile phone while driving?
- Taking unnecessary calls on holiday?
- Watching rubbish TV and wondering why?
- Snacking when you don't need to?
- Missing the opportunity to call someone you love?
- Worrying about stuff you can't control?
- Wasting time on social media?
- Putting stuff off in a way that makes you feel bad?

These are just some of the signs that you're being bossed by your own impulses.

Most of us think that this wonderfully evolved brain of ours is what allows us to be our best and allows us to thrive. And that is true. It is the conscious and deliberate attention of the Human brain that enables us to make better choices. But those choices I've just listed are neither conscious nor deliberate.

They probably don't even feel like choices. You just find yourself doing them – bypassing the Human brain in any of the decision-making. We usually find ourselves doing them because they are things we have repeated over and over again. We are simply more practised at doing them. Even though they might not be the most useful things to do, or even be any good for us, they are nevertheless easier because they have become habits and demand little, if any, Human-brain attention. The Human brain has surrendered all responsibility to our impulses and urges, relinquishing any effort needed for deliberation. As one client said to me recently, 'I know I could do it. It's just easier not to.'

To be better at anything we need the involvement of our extraordinary Human brain – to help us choose the most useful things to focus on and not be distracted or bossed into doing something else. Before I share ways to do that, and reveal how others have worked to resist being bossed, let's find out who's doing the bossing. Let me introduce you to:

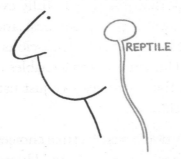

From the most adapted and cultivated brain to the most primeval – the Reptile brain is the oldest of them all. It is attached to the spinal column and the brain stem and acts as a motorway, carrying sensory messages from our body – particularly our gut and heart – to our brain and back again. A two-way street, it keeps us alive through all our non-conscious activities, busying itself with things we don't even think about: breathing, digestion, temperature regulation. The Reptile brain looks after our basic needs. Given the choice and in the right, comfortable conditions, it is happy doing nothing apart from those basics. Thankfully. In dodgy circumstances – unusual or unexpected situations – it will react very fast and instinctively, and as such is constantly alert, surveying the scene, looking out for one of the four Fs. Foe? Food? Friend? Or the other one starting with F? Whichever it is will cause an involuntary physical reaction that literally forces itself upon us: heart pumping, stomach disappearing into our boots or jumping into our throat, hands inadvertently shaking or sweating – releasing various hormones around our bodies. We are unable to stop this.

This is exactly what happened to Rachel when her boss opened the meeting in a way she was not expecting. Her Human brain was prepped and ready to control the situation. Suddenly she was confronted with a new circumstance and – before her Human brain had a chance to assess and make a choice – her Reptile brain sensed a potential foe and put her body into a state of alert, taking control. According to Rachel, as soon as her boss opened the meeting in that unexpected way, all rational thought left her and physical reactions took over. Actually, if we were to rerun the scene in slow motion, we would probably notice something happening even before Rachel's boss opened the meeting. If we were to zoom the camera in on the boss, I am willing to wager that something, however subliminal, in her physical presence in that room had already set off alarm bells in Rachel's primeval security system, be it a lack of eye contact, or no affirming smile or a defensive posture.

The Reptile brain may be primeval but, as such, it is incredibly experienced when it comes to sensing the unexpected. Its well-intentioned primitive impulse then takes over, shutting down any Human-brain involvement, which it deems unnecessary for Rachel's survival.

I work with many people who get infuriated when their physical reactions take over unexpectedly. Or, as Rachel now calls them, her 'well-intentioned primitive impulses'.

How does *your* Reptile brain show up? Do you:

- Go red?

- Shake?

- Find your voice cracks?

- Get butterflies?

- Find yourself unable to speak?

- Feel your heart thumping?

- Get hot?

- Go cold?

- Have a dry throat?

- Feel sick?

- Go tense?

- Lose colour?

- Get sweaty palms?

- Need the loo?

All these physical reactions demonstrate the Reptile brain in action – putting us on alert – reactions over which we have no control. The challenge for a lot of us is choosing how we respond to the sensations they cause. The Reptile brain reacts way before the Human brain.

In an experiment at the University of Iowa, card players were wired up for skin conductance (which climbs as stress increases, causing palms to sweat) and were asked to play a game where they could win or lose money depending on which card they selected from red and blue packs. The red packs were negatively rigged and, after turning over eighty cards, the players were able to explain what was wrong with the red pack. Their Human brains had assessed the information available from the eighty cards and made a decision. But, extraordinarily, the skin conductance equipment registered that their palms began sweating (the Reptile brain) when they reached for the red cards after only *ten* cards. It would take another seventy cards before their Human brains rationally understood the problem.

The Reptile brain prompts physical reactions with the sole intention of avoiding anything that threatens our survival. As soon as this happens, another brain gets involved.

THE DOG BRAIN

The Dog brain (as I refer to it) has been around almost as long as the Reptile. Unlike the Human brain, the Dog brain is a much simpler operator. It picks up the physical urges from the Reptile brain and responds impulsively and emotionally in three broad categories, which I describe as bark, cower and wag.

Sometimes these responses make sense and sometimes they don't. They all have positive intent and made much more sense thousands of years ago when they were critical to preserving our primitive survival – protecting us from extinction. The Dog brain, often semi-autonomously, is always interpreting situations. It is looking to do one of two things: minimize any potential threat or maximize any reward. It assesses in conjunction with the Reptile brain whether a particular situation or person is potentially dangerous (bark/cower) or worth approaching (wag). It does this very quickly and intuitively, comparing this current reality with all the past experiences it has remembered, and propelling us to move away from anything that is likely to do us harm – all done with positive intent, in service to our survival. The Dog brain (like the Reptile brain) is hardwired to assume that anything new or a surprise is a threat.

If you find yourself shouting inanely at a complete stranger from behind your steering wheel when they have decided to pinch the parking place you were patiently waiting for, that's your Dog brain barking. When you find yourself unexpectedly in the spotlight at work and are shocked and unable to respond, that's your Dog brain cowering. It's the Dog brain that impels us to say yes (wag) when we wish we had said no. I still have to work really hard at this. In fact, I have given my business partner permission to 'wag' his hand at me if he hears me 'wagging' at a client's request when we are already overstretched, rather than disappoint them. People I meet regularly find themselves saying yes to requests from their bosses, colleagues, family or friends, and then walk away asking themselves, 'Why the hell did I agree to that?' Answer: the Dog brain. It has decided that the reward they'll get from pleasing that person will on some level keep them safe and help them survive. These are all unconscious choices based on the emotion we feel rather than on rational thought (the Human brain).

The good news is that, just like dogs, the Dog brain can be trained to develop different responses or habits. Some dogs are more trainable than others, however. My own, actual dog, Kali, is excellent at coming when she is called and staying at heel if we are walking by a busy road. But if she spots a squirrel . . . *voom!*

In the same way, our Dog brain often responds so quickly we are not even conscious of it until it has happened.

Put simply, our three brains are in a perpetual tussle between conscious rational thought and faster impulses and urges. They are wired to intercommunicate constantly, up and down, up and down, with the aim of making as much of what we do as automatic as possible to conserve our energy. To become habits. Sometimes these habits are helpful and sometimes they are not.

Our three brains need to work as a team.

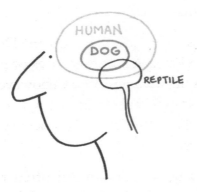

The Dog brain is the conduit between the Human and Reptile brains, keeping the information flowing freely so we can function at our best and make useful decisions. However, it is constantly assessing and interpreting, based on our past experiences, and will – if it deems necessary – jump into action (bark, cower or wag) in good faith and with positive intent to protect us, making a fast judgement ('if I involve the Human brain at this point it will be too slow, so you and me, Reptile, need to deal with this one before it's too late') and bypassing any rational thought the Human brain might have to offer.

For much of the time this is actually useful and even harmonious. Many aspects of our life are sensibly governed by the instincts we have been born with, and our intuitions and habits can be of great help to us in lots of situations.

The challenge is to allow our Reptile and Dog brains to run as much of our life as possible outside our conscious awareness, while at the same time remaining alert to those moments when this 'fast' operating system might benefit from a 'slow' and deliberate Human-brain override.

The following example, taken from my observations of a team in action, shows just how quickly the Reptile and Dog brains can combine and take over.

Barry was a jovial member of his team. I'd met him on many occasions before and had found him to be a positive, cheerful energy. His colleagues liked him. I had gone along to observe an off-site meeting in which the team were discussing how to usefully update each other on current projects and so maximize their time at meetings. One particular colleague, Philip, piped up about the benefits of the written update that he had done previously, and I noticed Barry start shifting in his seat. His face flushed, his jawline tightened and one of his legs began to pulse up and down under the table in an agitated fashion. Philip went into more detail, and I could see Barry fidget even more, rolling his eyes and looking around the room as his leg pulsed even faster under the table. Just as Philip was suggesting sending round a written update before the next meeting, Barry suddenly exploded, 'Please God, no! The last report you wrote was dreadful and made me want to vomit.'

I had watched as Barry's Reptile and then Dog brains reacted, taking the helm, as soon as mention was made of the previous report. Based on the memory of how the previous report had made him feel, Barry had exploded without any concern for the consequences. As Barry did so, Philip flushed to his roots (Reptile) and for the rest of the meeting didn't say another word (cowering Dog).

Barry had blurted emotionally. He hadn't made a considered choice. That sounds strange, I know. Surely our emotions are our choice. When people say to me, 'I'm furious because . . .', 'I'm stressed about . . .', or tell me that they're scared or even thrilled or excited by a possible situation, their Reptile and Dog brains are usually telling them something worth hearing. However, what I notice in them (and also in myself) is that, occasionally, the Reptile and Dog brains quickly and unhelpfully combine forces and, before we know it, overpower and boss the Human brain. One of my former teaching colleagues, Melinda, experienced this once at the end of a long school day.

Sometimes, after the final school bell had sounded, a ballooning mass of children would steam excitedly along the corridors, running to get outside and elbowing anyone who made the mistake of being in the way. This would generally mean one thing: a fight was about to take place. On this one occasion I saw several members of staff running towards the nucleus of the crowd to break it up. As I approached, I noticed a young teacher trying to persuade one of the main protagonists from continuing the fight – asking him to stop and walk away. She was doing a great job – remaining calm yet firm, her body confident and upright. She kept repeating the message: 'Leave him alone. You'll be the bigger person if you stop and turn away. Come on, don't get yourself into further trouble.' The child was completely ignoring her, straining to get at his opponent, the crowd jeering. This was the point when she lost it. It was as if she snapped into someone else. Flushing red, she shouted in his face, 'DID YOU NOT HEAR WHAT I SAID?' He held her stare and said nothing. The point of focus was now the teacher and the child eyeballing one another, noses almost touching – more spectacle for the crowd. At that point a senior member of staff pushed through, gently put her hand on the young teacher's shoulder and whispered in her ear, 'Melinda . . . you're the adult.'

The pull of someone else's Dog brain inviting you to bark can be immense. The teacher's Human brain had been desperately trying to remain in control, rationally reminding her that she was the teacher – her role was to take care of both the situation and the children involved. She knew that. However, there was a stronger, competing urge. An urge to survive. As I watched, her initial calm stance had become more and more rigid as she edged further in towards the fight. Her Reptile brain, sensing a possible defeat if she couldn't control the children, had alerted her Dog brain to the threat. Reptile and Dog had stepped in to take over from the Human-brain involvement: *This is not the time for rational thought. It isn't working. You're being humiliated in front of pupils you teach. Leave it to us. He's ignoring you. YOU need to win. You need to bark louder.* So she had barked louder. It had taken someone else's Human brain to come in and rescue the situation.

Someone else's Dog brain can feel like the pull of a very strong rip tide. We want to keep our feet on the sand and hold tight, but instead we are sucked in by a force that seems much stronger than us. Coming up for air after we have been thrown around underwater can leave us feeling confused, disorientated, shocked and a bit bedraggled. That's what it felt like for Darren.

Darren is my dog walker. He is very gentle and caring and Kali, my dog, loves him. One afternoon Darren arrived to pick up Kali in a rather shaken state. He described an incident that had happened in the local park that morning when he was walking the other dogs he looks after.

As he was playing with the four dogs in his care, a guy

strode up and kicked out at one of them. This incensed Darren.

'We had a short exchange of harsh words. He accused me of having "too many fucking dogs". I told him, "I'm a dog walker – what do you expect?"

'He ignored me and just ranted on and on. What did I do? I found myself marching the dogs away to safety. I could hear the bloke shouting across the park at me. I got back to the car, locked them in and then, guess what? I ran back to find that man. When I caught up with him, I asked what his problem was and, before I knew it, I'd wrestled him to the ground, was grappling with him, shouting, "If you try kicking one of my dogs again, you'll have me to deal with." I couldn't stop myself.

'It's really shaken me up and I've been running it through my head for the last couple of hours. I wish I'd had a more adult response. I haven't had a fight like that since I was at school. I'm in my thirties, for God's sake.'

You can hear Darren's Human brain coming into play as he attempts to assess how on earth that happened.

When the urge from the Reptile comes, the Dog brain's inclination is to be impulsive – instigating a movement of some sort. When it impels us to jump out of the way of a moving car, we are grateful. It's the gearbox between Reptile and Human – between the primitive urge from the Reptile and the considered response of the Human. Darren could have stopped at any point as he walked back to the car. However, the Dog brain's sense of justice had been violated, Darren became fired up by indignation – and his Dog brain's determination to be right took control.

As I write this, I'm taken back to a moment in the school playground when I was thirteen.

There had been an ongoing argument between my friend Suzanne and a girl called Judy. I remember Judy approaching us and telling Suzanne – in front of everyone and in a very humiliating fashion – exactly what she thought of her. Judy then turned on her heel and smugly walked away, beaming from ear to ear. I never have and never would consider myself a violent person in any way, but as soon as I saw the hurt in Suzanne's face, I found myself marching after Judy. Grabbing her arm, I spun her around, screamed 'How dare you?' and promptly slapped her around the face. I then legged it and locked myself in the loo. What had I done? I remained there petrified until a teacher came and found me.

There's nothing like a feeling of injustice to spark the impulsive Dog brain into action. Seeing Judy smile after humiliating Suzanne propelled me to take revenge. It felt good to stand up publicly for my wronged friend. That satisfying impulse to lash out bypassed any intervention from my Human brain that could have warned me of the likely consequences of hitting a fellow pupil: a serious punishment from the school, as well as having to face my shocked and very disappointed parents.

My business partner, Simon, is probably one of the most rational people I know. Last year we were in an airport lounge at Heathrow, waiting to fly to Mexico, when our flight was called. Building work was ongoing so all the usual signage had been removed. We asked someone at the desk for directions to the gate and she told us, and around a dozen other passengers, to turn left out of the lounge. We ended up walking for about ten minutes in the wrong direction before we were eventually put right. By now the gate was closing and we had to jog to make the flight.

We just made it to the gate in time and, as we went through, my 'rational' business partner very politely asked the steward at the desk to let his manager know that it would have been helpful if there had been a sign telling us the correct way to get there.

The steward replied very abruptly, 'There was a sign, sir.'

'No, there wasn't actually,' Simon replied, still polite and supported by nods from the other passengers.

After a few more exchanges the steward, dismissively and without looking up, said, 'No, you're wrong. There is a sign.' He was so off-hand that I remember thinking, *Whoops. I know what happens now.*

I saw Simon's demeanour change – almost in slow motion – as his Reptile brain prepared his body for an attack and his Dog brain strained to persuade him to bark. The tussle with his Human brain was almost visible. I could nearly hear the growl!

'Right,' he declaimed, 'what was a passing comment has

now turned into an official complaint. And that complaint is about you.'

He turned to the steward's colleagues. 'I can tell you are embarrassed and feeling let down by his appalling service. I leave it to you to help your colleague reflect on how he might have handled that better.'

Not exactly an assault, but vicious nonetheless.

As we walked down to the plane, Simon's Reptile and Dog simply faded away and the controlled, rational business partner returned.

'I wish I hadn't been quite so harsh,' he confessed. Too late.

These are all examples of what I call 'Gut to Gob'. Many clients like using this phrase to acknowledge when their Reptile and Dog brains take the helm and steer them to a place they hadn't necessarily chosen. A Gut to Gob moment can feel good, but there can also be consequences.

Gut is Reptile. You can't stop it happening. Similarly, you can't prevent your Dog brain reacting to that gut feeling. You can't stop Gut to Dog. But you *can* stop Gut to Gob. If you choose to. The challenge is to slow down your response time so your Human brain has the chance to make a choice rather than leave the response in the less safe hands of your Reptile or Dog.

Being aware of these three brains and the way they interplay is hugely helpful to the people I work with.

Understanding which brain is taking charge is often the springboard for them as they set out on their 'be better' journey. They recognize how quickly their Reptile and Dog brains can take over, and they become more familiar with the signs that this is happening. Is it a racing heart? A red face? Are they suddenly talking faster or not talking at all? Knowing that three brains are involved in steering each of our choices and decisions is a simple, fun way of understanding what is happening. I have clients who find it a useful common language to have in their teams – and with their families. I witnessed a team member have a bit of an unhelpful 'blurt' in a team day and then almost immediately say, 'Apologies, that was my Dog brain. What I really meant to say was . . .' This allowed everyone to smile – including her – the moment passed more quickly, and she had an opportunity to take back control and choose how she wanted to express herself; in other words, to involve her Human brain.

Involving and aligning all three brains helps us to get better faster and with less effort. It is also more fun, as the inevitable lapses can be more easily laughed off as short-term victories for the Reptile and Dog. We need the Human brain to help us become better. Our Dog and Reptile brains are *always* a factor in how well it can do that. Clients who make the fastest progress are the ones who are able to quickly recognize when they are being bossed by their own impulses, and have practical ways to pause, be more considered when they want to and make better choices.

The Three Brains

Reptile	Physical response (body): The oldest and simplest part of the brain, it helps us stay alive, controls basic survival functions, looks out for the four Fs.
Dog	Emotional response (mood): Helps us survive, serves the Reptile brain, is impulsive and intuitive, and looks to reduce threat (move away) by barking and cowering, or maximize reward (move towards) by wagging.
Human	Rational response (mind): Helps us thrive by creating, relating, focusing, concentrating, problem-solving and making considered choices.

HOW THE REPTILE AND DOG PULL RANK

When something unexpected or novel happens, we will always react first with a physical sensation.

A split second later, almost simultaneously, our intuition (Dog brain) interprets these sensations and reacts accordingly – threat? Or reward?

Those two have now taken over, pulling rank on any conscious thought from the Human brain, which then surrenders control, impeding our ability to think rationally.

THE BRAIN GAME

Which brain is in charge, reptile, dog or human, when you:

	Reptile	Dog	Human
Go red			
Have butterflies in your stomach			
Say yes a lot and wish you hadn't			
Bypass lunch			
Go in a bus lane when you're allowed			
Don't go in a bus lane although you're allowed			
Look at your phone during a meeting			

Choose a longer route rather
than sit in traffic

Spend time creating a plan

Work on the pros and cons
of a decision

Lose concentration

Buy something you regret as
soon as you get home

Start shaking

For the Human brain to function at its best, it needs the
Dog and Reptile brains to be in harmony with it. Not
bossing it. I see these brains as three characters on a
stage – each with a different and crucial role to play in
helping us perform at our best. When all three brains
work together, as an ensemble, we create more choice for
ourselves. We can do this better when we manage our
energy.

Our Five Energies

Body Energy

Mood Energy

Mind Energy

Purpose Energy

People Energy

3.

'I felt depressed and slightly defeated – low energy – no real desire for the year ahead – generally looking up a hill. Could I really be bothered to do this any more? I wasn't sure I could, or even if I wanted to. I wasn't sleeping. I was feeling belittled and unappreciated. My weight suffered, my health suffered, I was exercising too little.

I was giving more and more at work and less and less at home. More and more time at work with people who had all bought into the pace and way of working, and my family were saying, 'This is utterly ridiculous. What the hell are you doing? Why are you putting up with this?' This culminated on holiday when I was sitting at the pool doing emails and my husband snatched the iPad out of my hands and threw it in the pool. 'If you are just going to work all holiday, Beverley, we are going home tomorrow.' I spent the rest of the day on top of a mountain in tears – I didn't want to do this any more, I'd lost my mojo. My marriage was falling apart. I had to do something.'

Beverley's three brains were in turmoil as the Reptile fought for its need for sleep, the Dog didn't know whether to bark, wag or cower, and all the time the Human brain was whirring away, trying to get emails done and becoming more and more unproductive.

A lot of us can relate to that feeling of turmoil. For some, it's all too familiar.

Most of the people I work with are trying to choose the best way to respond to the competing demands that their lives throw at them. On a macro level that might be being there for their children; working; looking after parents and siblings; trying to fit in the shopping. On a micro level, competing demands might mean juggling priorities in the space of a few hours – preparing a key document, answering emails, attending constant meetings, inspiring those you lead, being available for any urgent requests – all so you can leave early to attend a parents' evening that starts at 4 p.m.

The question is how do we get out of this turmoil?

The answer is to do with our energy. Actually, that should read *energies*.

Five performance energies that we all have access to and which are fundamental in helping us be at our best: body energy, mood energy, mind energy, purpose energy and people energy. If we think about our three brains as being the main characters on our stage, these five energies are the supporting cast waiting in the wings, readily available to play their part if we choose to pay attention

to them. The success and effectiveness of the performance of our three brains is dependent on this supporting
cast.

The cast list looks like this:

Starring	Supporting Cast
Reptile brain	Body energy
Dog brain	Mood energy
Human brain	Mind energy
	Purpose energy
	People energy

HOW OUR ENERGIES SUPPORT OUR BRAINS

How we manage these different energies has an enormous
influence on our ability to choose.

In every area of our lives there appears to be not only a
growing desire to achieve more in less time but also a
pressure to do it all really well. I often meet clients when
they are about to go on holiday, racing around at break-
neck speed to make sure they have completed everything
they need to do and set others up for success, hoping
that they don't 'arrive on holiday broken', as one client said
to me recently. They tend to return saying something like, 'It

took me the first three days to recover. I wasn't much fun to be with and the last two days of the holiday were about gearing myself up to return.'

As we all race around trying to achieve everything and achieve it well, there is a constant dialogue between our three brains and the five energies. When we have ways to manage these different energies, it makes it easier for our Reptile and Dog brains to support the Human brain in all its extraordinary functions. It is the Human brain that takes on the deliberate effort required to focus on making better choices. That effort uses up energy, so having ways to support that effort is vital.

I have worked with many people to help them get the most from their energies to support that effort. Informed by the practices of high performers from the arts, the military and sport, and having now worked with hundreds of clients, I have discovered that if you manage those energies in a specific order, it can make a significant impact on your ability to be your best. Whether you are the CEO of a global company, a teacher or a politician, the order matters. And here it is.

Before anything else, high performers make a point of looking after their *body energy*. This supports their Reptile brain. When they do this they feel in much better shape to generate the most useful *mood energy*. This calms their Dog brain, which, in turn, enables them to focus their *mind energy* on what matters and get the best from their Human brain. We generate these three energies from within ourselves. The other two vital sources of energy – *purpose*

56

energy and people energy – are generated from connecting with others.

So, how was the order playing out for Beverley?

Firstly, her *body energy* was clearly low. She wasn't sleeping well, she wasn't exercising and her health was suffering. This in turn made it harder for her to control her emotions, 'mood energy', and she fell victim to a feeling of being defeated and unappreciated. In this kind of depleted and negative state, the mind energy required to focus on choosing a different, more useful action depends hugely on having enough body energy and *mood energy*. Beverley had very little of either. As a consequence, she slipped easily into a more familiar action – working through her emails – to feel like she was achieving some sort of progress. She had lost her will (her 'mojo') – the meaning from which she had derived her *purpose energy* – and, by burying herself in emails, cut herself off from any connection and fun with her family and that boost of *people energy*.

Beverley hadn't gone on holiday with the intention of putting her marriage under so much strain; she just found herself in a downward spiral, trying to find a way through her increasing and competing demands. She was making herself unwell.

It's essential to have ways to manage each of our energies better to cope with life's increasing demands. To help us to feel, be and choose better.

Our Five Energies

Body Energy

Mood Energy

Mind Energy

Purpose Energy

People Energy

4.

CHOOSE TO USE YOUR BODY

Body energy is the first thing to consider when setting out on the journey to be better. It is the foundation for the other four energies and consequently strengthens our ability to make better choices. Together, my business partner and I combined our own insights from our performance backgrounds with those from our work with high performers. We then constructed a method built around four vital pillars:

Sleep

Hydration

Exercise

Diet

Welcome to the SHED method.

To maintain a good level of body energy, you need a sensible balance of all four: sleep, hydration, exercise and diet – your SHED.

Looking after your SHED gives your Reptile brain sufficient body energy so that your Dog and Human brains work well together. In simple terms, sleep, hydration, exercise and diet offer a way of managing your Reptile brain. Even quite habitual activities can become a struggle if we are tired, thirsty, out of condition or hungry.

We function at our best when we have the fuel we need to perform – like other things in our lives. One of my family's traditions when I was a child was the annual summer trip to Cornwall. I would get excited as the day approached and never more so than the night before, when my father would open the bonnet of our old Vauxhall Viva to test the oil. I would sit and watch through the front window as he extracted the spindly metal dipstick to show how much oil was in the engine. A thick black oil mark indicated whether or not it was at the recommended level. If it was too low, he would add more oil so that the engine would work efficiently during the long drive and the journey would be completed without any disasters.

It seems absolutely basic (and it is), but when we're busy or striving to achieve, we often fail to pay attention to the fundamental things that make a huge difference to how good we feel and how well we perform. If you make a conscious effort to pay more attention to your body energy, you can find simple ways to feel better and achieve more. Personally, I know I find it especially hard to function well if I don't get enough sleep. If I don't address this need, my body shouts louder – often in the form of swollen tonsils. Because I know the quality of my sleep matters to me, over the last few years I have been investigating what makes the biggest difference to that quality. I now recognize that my sleep is less restful if my evening meal is too close to bedtime. And if my meal includes carbohydrates, I wake up particularly foggy the next day. I sometimes choose to ignore these insights because I'm prioritizing something else, but I know that, to be on top form, I need to pay attention to these factors. For my business partner, it's exercise. For him this usually means waking up very early (abnormally early in my view!) and running (again, in my view) an abnormally long way. Both my husband and my daughter get grumpy if they haven't eaten. It's all individual.

A few years ago I was staying in a hotel in Los Angeles

and got into conversation with a woman sitting nearby. We were both enjoying a bit of quiet time beside the pool in the sun, on our own, reading – me a novel, her something on a laptop. We were simultaneously distracted as a clearly frustrated mother looked to persuade her children to leave the pool and go for lunch. The children – who, it wasn't difficult to deduce, were called Troy and Jessica – were having none of it. They were having a great time doing underwater handstands and screaming with laughter as they tried to duck each other. Their mum was standing at the edge, holding towels out and becoming increasingly annoyed. The woman next to me caught my eye and gave one of those *So glad that's not me* looks. I smiled in agreement. We clearly both wanted the children to do what their mother asked and soon, so that we could continue enjoying some peace in the sun. When the mother had stormed off indoors, presumably in the hope they would feel guilty and chase her, they remained steadfastly in the pool and continued to play. My co-conspirator looked over and said, 'I hope they get hungry soon. I flew in three hours ago and this wasn't part of the plan.'

We got talking. It transpired that Myra was in LA on business. She spent a lot of her time travelling the world for work. This was what she called a 'recovery moment', and was crucial for her. Myra told me that a key part of her keeping on top of things, despite all the travel, was to factor in a recovery day after a long flight. In her words: 'It gives me time to catch up, unpack, take calls in my PJs and know that I can stride in the next day up to speed and feeling fresh.'

This made absolute sense to me, but how did it go down at work?

'At first I would receive some raised eyebrows from my senior colleagues, but I know that I'll be better because of that day, and I am. They now accept that it is an important part of my routine if I'm going to be at my best.' She smiled. 'And some have even started doing it themselves and comment on the difference it makes to their energy.'

Myra's practice of a recovery day has remained with me ever since, and I too now factor in recovery time when I travel. Those colleagues of hers initially frowned on the practice, no doubt deeming it selfish of Myra. However, when they did it themselves, they realized the benefits almost immediately. I believe that the word *selfish* gets a bad press. And I now regularly ask clients what they would do if they were to be *properly selfish*.

I use this phrase as a means of helping people find a way through the apparent paradox that sometimes the best way to look after others is to look after yourself first.

It's also worth noting that those high performers who develop routines and rituals to help them be better agree that being properly selfish matters. In other words, looking after *you* is central to choosing to be better both for yourself and for others.

So, when it comes to *your* body energy, and looking after *your* SHED, how properly selfish are you?

This question elicits a variety of reactions from clients. Having *properly* and *selfish* in the same phrase feels counterintuitive. It seems indulgent, yet at the same time there's a tingle of relief that someone has mentioned it as a possibility. But looking after oneself in order to be better at something or better for someone else can be crucial. On a plane, for example, we are told – in the event of an emergency – to place our own oxygen mask on first before helping our children. That way we will be in better shape to look after them and help them with theirs. Selfish or sensible? Apparently this procedure is very hard for a parent to do, which is completely understandable – the Dog brain is telling us to do the opposite. And in my work, I see just how hard it is for many people to invest in the concept of proper selfishness.

However, for those who do manage it, three things appear to really help them:

1. They know it matters.

2. They create the time and a routine.

3. They try things out to discover what works best for them.

Take, for instance, the case of one of my clients, Susan, who described herself as feeling tired, slightly numb, and not as creative as she had once been. When I asked how she might be properly selfish more regularly, she looked at me with a slightly bemused expression, as if I'd sworn or hadn't really understood what she had just said. 'I haven't any time to do any more,' she told me. 'I just want to feel differently about what I am doing. I want to feel more creative, have some fresh ideas, feel less exhausted.'

When we next met, she said the phrase *properly selfish* had remained with her over the following few days and she'd been discussing it with her husband. When she asked him what it meant to him, he immediately replied, 'Playing football on Wednesday night and Sunday morning. Without that I'd be unbearable.' They then had a really interesting discussion about what her equivalent would be.

Her answer? She realized that her idea of being properly selfish was burying herself in a book when she felt she could. She hadn't read a book for pleasure for ages, and she missed it. 'Holidays are great,' she said, 'because I allow myself to indulge in as many as I can get through.'

Having time to read had begun to feel like 'nice to do on holiday' rather than 'an investment in me to be better', particularly as, since her promotion, she felt that any spare time at home should be spent with her family. So she decided to experiment with the notion of being more properly selfish. She decided to commit to spending one evening a month with her friends at a book club that they had been trying to persuade her to join for some time.

Joining the club worked on many levels. It was once a month, at a regular time, and there were others involved, so reading that month's book was her commitment not only to herself but to them too, which helped her stick to it.

Susan had always thought that focusing on herself was OK – as long as she had achieved everything else she needed to do first. It was always lower down the list than whatever was happening at work or with her family. Her approach shifted when she began to realize that investing in herself actually allowed her to be more effective in everything else. She enjoyed her 'reading times', they refuelled her, and she began to experiment with other properly selfish habits too.

Another client, Kevin, would always use his journey home on the 7.15 train from Waterloo as an opportunity to complete any unfinished work, despite having already worked a long day in the office. The one-hour journey back became an extension of his working day. He became incredibly proficient at setting up his portable office on board – feeling a strange sense of satisfaction if he had started work before the train left the platform. Similarly, on the early-morning commute, his portable office enabled him to 'bash out some emails' and set things up for the day. It had become a habit.

'I've realized that all I do is work, arrive home later than I'd like, still thinking about work, miss the kids' bedtime, collapse, wake up, leave home and start again,' he told me. 'I don't know what else to do – it seems the only way to stay on top of it all.'

When we discussed how he could be more properly selfish, he confessed that he would like to use his travel time to relax rather than feel compelled to work. He mentioned that he had always wanted to learn French and agreed to experiment with his commute and how he might use that time differently. He invested in a great set of headphones and began to use the hour at both ends of the day (which he called 'moi' time) to sit back and be a student

68

again. He discovered that spending an hour focused on something he really wanted to learn meant he arrived at work much more eager to focus on his team. He also found he returned home with much more energy to devote to his family. His increased efficiency during the day meant he was also able to catch an earlier train at least once a week to see the kids before bed.

I am a big fan of Adele – not only because of her extra-ordinary voice, but also because of the raw honesty in her songs and the way she talks to her fans during her sets. When I saw her in concert, she had such a great connection and openness with her fans that it was as if we were all sitting in a pub, catching up. In one of her chats she shared something that could have been lifted straight from this section: 'The most important thing to me in my life is being a mum. And I'm really important to myself too – because if I don't look after myself and love myself, I can't be a good mum.'

Find out what works for you. Everyone's different. You might need more sleep, whereas your colleague might need to eat more regularly. A client may say at the start of our session that they need to find a way forward with a relationship, a strategic decision, a particular challenge or the way they are feeling, and it often comes down to some-thing as simple as 'I need to sleep more to make progress' or 'It didn't help that I hadn't eaten that morning.' It's important to experiment or, as I say, 'act and learn' to find your properly selfish investment to keep you strong for yourself and for others – and make it non-negotiable. When we look after our SHED and pay attention to our sleep, hydration, exercise and diet, we provide our Reptile brain with the body energy it needs to do what it does best: looking after our basic needs and keeping us alive.

Let's look in more detail at each of the elements in turn.

LEEP

(THIS INCLUDES REST AND RELAXATION)

For some warped reason people often display great pride when they discuss how much they've achieved on next to no sleep. It's like they've entered into a competition, akin to Monty Python's 'Four Yorkshiremen' sketch: 'You think that's tough? I got barely more than three hours last night because I was working on a document till 3 a.m. and still managed to get up and fire off ten emails before dropping the kids at school and getting to work.'

Similarly, people tend to admire those colleagues who appear to thrive on less than the average amount of sleep, believing that it's a strength. Margaret Thatcher was lauded by her backbenchers for her four hours' sleep a night, and I don't recall her dispelling the rumour. More recently, Bill Clinton apparently presided over the White House on about five hours' sleep a night, and people were in awe of this. He, on the other hand was rather more realistic: 'In my long political career,' he said, 'most of the mistakes I made, I made when I was too tired. You make better decisions when you're not too tired.'

The findings of the 2012 Great British Sleep Survey support this statement. They suggest that when men and women are deprived of sleep, the three most affected areas are their energy levels, relationships and mood. The survey reports that, compared to people who get the optimum amount of sleep (seven to eight hours a night), those who regularly don't get enough sleep are seven times more likely to feel helpless, five times more likely to feel alone and three times more likely to struggle to concentrate or be productive. I can relate to all of those.

Sheena found this out at huge cost. She had gained a promotion within an international company more quickly than she had expected. She was ambitious and was delighted to have this opportunity. It came with a lot more responsibility but, after a discussion with her husband, she accepted. She was excited initially and attacked the role with gusto. But the work ballooned. More work meant more meetings, more travel and more time away from her young family. She started to feel that she wasn't on top of her emails and her workload in general. To try to take back control, she would arrive at work earlier and earlier, and leave later and later, carrying even more work home with her to do into the night – once she had helped put the children to bed. She felt overwhelmed and unable to think straight, and her workload just seemed to keep growing. As it all spiralled, she started getting home after the children had gone to bed, something that, perversely, made her feel relieved as she could get straight on with her work. Something had to give. After five months of trying to stay on top of everything both at work and at home, she was feeling unwell, had lost all motivation, found no enjoyment in anything, and finally was signed off work by her doctor. That's when we met.

'My normal routine was to work at the dining table while Sam, wonderfully, would cook and put our dinner in front of me,' she told me. 'This enabled me to work on as I ate and carry on through to bedtime. That tended to be late and was normally dictated by whenever I had finished dotting the "i"'s and crossing the "t"'s on a document on my iPad in bed.'

Many people believe that in order to prove they can manage it all, and be taken seriously, they have to work harder and longer. This is particularly true of women returning to work after maternity leave (myself included). They worry about being seen as less efficient because they now have other responsibilities. I have seen both men and women (but mostly the latter) who, once they have a family, have chosen to return to a four-day week but end up doing the equivalent of a five-day week to assuage their guilt or prove their value. Their Dog brains are madly wagging, saying yes to things for fear of being thought of as less committed or valuable now that they aren't full-time — and neglecting themselves as a consequence.

Actress Kim Cattrall suffered from acute insomnia caused by 'the perfect storm of grief, work pressure and the menopause'. She retrained her brain and body through pre-sleep rituals like taking a bath and banishing electronic devices from the bedroom. Only sleep and sex were permitted in bed. Her mind became clearer and her energy levels close to restored. Work had become her child and she'd let it rule her life. She said 'The big positive from the whole experience was releasing. I don't do enough things for the heck of it. When I do things for the heck of it, I find myself in a very happy place. She defines 'the heck of it' as 'a day to be funny, fart around, relax, hang'. I have a few clients who find the-heck-of-it days essential. They call them 'who-cares afternoons', 'no-plan days' or, my favourite: 'oh-sod-it sessions'.

The neuroscientist David Rock calls it **downtime** and describes it as 'anything non-goal-focused: reading, a mundane task like washing the dishes, or just literally sitting on the couch, zoning out. This is allowing your mind to wander and reflect. This will allow your brain time to recover, and you'll get an added bonus: You're allowing space for your unconscious connections to come to the surface, to solve complex problems.'

After she had been signed off sick, Sheena went back to basics, first by establishing a new sleep routine:

> I set myself a regular (earlier) bedtime, switched off all technology one hour before that and read. To start with I found this immensely difficult. One thing that helped was changing what I would read at that time. Before bed I stopped reading anything work-related and instead chose something light. I had a few novels – fiction, mostly – that I'd been bought as gifts in the past and had been meaning to read, so I started on those. At first I would berate myself, 'You have so much to do. Why on earth are you pretending you have the time to read this!'

This was despite her being signed off work and not having to 'do' anything. It was an old habit of hers, believing she could only relax when she had completed everything.

'Eventually, through deliberate persistence,' she said, 'both these changes made sleeping much easier and, frankly, more relaxed. Focusing on sleep first enabled me to start to refuel. I also began eating better and more regularly. I focused on enjoying the meal (and telling Sam that!) rather than trying to do other things at the same time.'

Three months later Sheena was heading back to work, buoyed by her refuelling and with a new evening diet and sleep rhythm hopefully embedded. I say *hopefully*, because it was about to be severely tested. This is how Sheena described it:

Initially I found it very seductive to return to old habits. We had planned for the pull of this temptation – especially as there was so much work to get up to speed on. But I noticed that when I did feel compelled to step away from the new habit, my energy levels dipped, my clarity of thought suffered and I was more reluctant to make decisions. Touching on that 'old feeling' was enough for me to power up my new rules.

When Sheena returned to work, she confronted the same environment and the same pressures as before. Her challenge was to maintain her new habits when faced with the same old situation. You can't completely eradicate an old habit. It is always there, waving at you, tempting you to come back when the familiar triggers are around – emails to respond to, meetings to attend, more and more decisions to be made. Thankfully though, the months away from work had given Sheena a chance to embed her new evening routine. She was now much better at recognizing and resisting the pull of her Dog brain as it tried to get her to do what she always did in those high-pressured work situations and work longer, even if that made her less efficient.

Getting enough sleep helps us perform better at anything. It improves our ability to concentrate, to be creative, to focus and to make choices. A lack of it addles our mental capacity. For example, studies have shown that after just one night without proper sleep, soldiers lose 30 per cent of their cognitive capability. By contrast, a twenty-minute nap can increase a NASA pilot's productivity by

34 per cent. Interestingly, neither of these statistics has any impact on 100 per cent of the teenagers in my house.

Arianna Huffington, the creator of the worldwide web success the *Huffington Post*, made headlines across the globe when she said, 'To be successful we need to sleep our way to the top.' Of course, she knew full well the attention she would draw by saying that, but she was being deadly serious when she went on to say that sleep is the secret to success. 'The most basic shift we can make in redefining success in our lives,' she said, 'has to do with our strained relationship with sleep.' Sheena agrees.

So how can we get the most out of our sleep to boost our body energy? Below are some sleep practices – and some tips on rest and taking breaks generally – that others have tried and that made a difference to their body energy.

See if any of them work for you:

- I've started going to bed and getting up at the same time every day.

- I set a go-to-bed alarm as well as a get-up alarm.

- I make sure I have some 'me time' in the evening.

- I shut down all devices one hour before I go to bed.

- When I struggle to sleep, I remember that rest is good too.

- I've made my bedroom dark, quiet and cool – a high-quality sleep environment for high-quality sleep.

- I make sure that supper is done and dusted two to three hours before bed, and I have no caffeine from twelve hours before I go to sleep.

- I take a fifteen- to twenty-minute nap every lunchtime. I call them 'smart naps'. They help me focus in the afternoon.

- I bought a velvet armchair for my office at work to create a personal zone in there. My desk is for work, phone and emails; my armchair is for 'me time' – thinking, resting or simply creating an energy change.

- I leave a bag outside my bedroom door. I put my worries in there for the night, to separate them from my sleep. I then look at them in the morning and decide which ones I will pick up and deal with.

- I take a bath in the evening and banish all distracting electronic devices from the bedroom.

YDRATION

I'm going to start here with a very extreme example of high performance. Not because I expect you all to down tools and become Olympic champions, but because it's a clear indicator of the importance of water.

Great Britain has a wonderful history of rowing success at the Olympic Games. A member of our team, double Olympic gold medallist Steve Williams, gave me a tour of one of the fulcrums of that success, Leander Club in Henley. As you enter the building, practically the first thing you see is a huge board full of names. These are the Olympic medal winners. As Steve explained to me, 'The gold medal winners are written in gold. Bronze and silver medallists are the ones written in black.' Clearly winning is the only option. As soon as you walk into the building, there is immediately a focus on success and being better than the rest. The other thing that struck me, as I watched the rowers warm up, practise, warm down and even socialize, was that they all carried a water bottle. It was as if they were surgically attached. I asked Steve why. He explained:

> Every morning the rowers are tested in several physiological parameters to monitor their performance and recovery. They measure resting heart rate; body weight; sleep hours and quality. Blood and urine are also tested for urea and hydration. All are important, but Jürgen [the coach] puts the greatest emphasis on the hydration score as the key measure for the body's readiness to perform at its highest level on that day. So everyone makes sure they have a water bottle on them at all times, and they sip water continually.

One would assume that this rehydration is simply a physical thing, that these athletes are trained to replace sweat and maintain their physical prowess. However, according to a study carried out by Loughborough University in 2015, 'Dehydration can also result in impaired mental functioning, changes in mood and reductions in concentration, alertness and short-term memory.'

When I think about the importance of hydration, I think of Val. I accept that hers is an extreme example, but it is nevertheless a very real example and a reminder of what can happen when we ignore warning signs.

Val was a forty-something headteacher and, through her dedication to and passion for leading a great school, was usually the last to leave the building every day and available on email all weekend. She had got into a pattern where food and drink were constantly sidelined. She might grab a sandwich to eat on the go, but that was about it. All of this was affecting her body. She often felt a niggle in her stomach and rarely felt the need to visit the toilet – both clear signs of constipation. Indeed, it seemed quite normal to her to go a whole week without a trip to the bathroom, and when that same niggle became a pain, she ignored it, thinking, *It'll be fine.*

It wasn't like this was a new experience, either. She had twice before visited her GP when these issues presented themselves, and the doctor told her she was dehydrated and that she needed to drink more. After following this advice for perhaps a week or two, Val soon fell back into her old habits: *A cup of tea should cover the hydration*, she thought – then she'd have nothing for the rest of the day. How wrong she was.

It was the end of a summer term. Val was dealing with

everything work threw at her while ignoring that normal 'niggle' and constipation. Term finished on a Friday and the next morning in the supermarket, with no work to occupy her, she realized the extent of the pain she was in. She abandoned her trolley and hobbled into an out-of-hours clinic. Once there, she was whisked into an ambulance and off to the hospital, where an extensive course of rehydration began. She was in hospital for four days while she underwent this, and at the same time had to take a course of antibiotics because she had developed diverticulitis, a disease that infects the pockets of the bowel. She was told that she would also need an operation at a later stage to clear the polyps that had taken root in there. Consultant after consultant told her that her condition had undoubtedly been exacerbated by dehydration.

That time in hospital gave Val a huge wake-up call. Thankfully she has now fully recovered, but only because, when she left hospital, she drank the recommended amount of water every day. This meant she had to create a daily practice to help her remember to do it. When she came to see me, just after she'd left hospital, she admitted that drinking water was not something she enjoyed, and she said that she'd probably find it very hard.

We discussed the value of having a buddy to help build the practice, and she chose to work in partnership with her PA. We agreed that the PA would place a jug of water on Val's desk every morning, and that Val had to drink it all by the end of the day.

At the next session, though, Val admitted that she hadn't

made much progress with her new drinking habit. The jug was often still very full at the end of a working day. This was interesting, as she really did have a strong desire to stay well. Yet she hadn't made any progress on drinking more. We looked at making some adjustments. There was a specific glass she had at home that she liked to drink out of because of its shape, so she decided to bring it to work. The PA would fill up this glass all the time. Together they created a practice whereby Val would take a sip of water from this glass before answering the phone and before answering the door. If, by the end of the school day, Val hadn't emptied the jug, she would pour the remainder in a bottle and take it with her in the car to finish before she arrived home. She liked swigging from the bottle while she drove.

These adjustments worked a lot better, and the practice evolved over time as she began to drink more. If she had to attend a meeting off-site, her PA would check she had a bottle of water with her and would put a cheeky 'water' symbol next to the time of the meeting in her diary. According to Val, having someone at work supporting her and being regularly reminded in a fun way really helped her take her hydration seriously. Not only did this new regime reverse the condition that had seen Val hospitalized, but she also began to notice that her energy levels grew, which enabled her to achieve what she needed to during the day rather than taking work home over the weekend. She now drinks water without any prompting. In her words, 'It's now part of what I do.'

Here are a few examples of hydration practices that others have tried and say make a difference to their body energy. See if any of them work for you:

- Where I go, my water bottle goes – always.

- Every morning I make sure there's a jug of water on the desk. I have to finish it by the time I go home.

- I have allotted three days a week as caffeine/alcohol-free days.

- I have set H_2O alarms on my phone for every two hours.

- I put a large glass of water by my bed and drink it as soon as I wake up.

- I have no caffeine after midday.

- I make myself practise asking for mint tea rather than a double espresso!

Now, take a break and have a drink of water before we move on to . . .

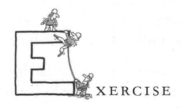

XERCISE

Physical movement and exercise pump oxygen through the body and brain, boosting brainpower and releasing hormones that can shift our mood. Physical movement is part of who we are. As humans we are meant to move.

Back in the savannah, moving was a positive thing to do. Our survival depended on it. We moved to find food, safety, a new mate. We are hard-wired to have a positive response to movement. However, as we have evolved, we have found ourselves with fewer reasons to move while our ever more complex world demands more from the Human brain. We easily convince ourselves that we don't have time to exercise or move if we are to achieve all we want in a day. Exercise and movement seem to have become something we do when we have time rather than a key aspect of helping us to both feel and be better.

A recent study at Iowa State University has shown how just going for a short walk can have a beneficial impact on our mood and motivation. The study assessed the joviality, vigour, attentiveness and self-assurance of students who went on a tour as a group, walking around campus, and revealed that these students reported a more positive mood than those who spent the same period of time sitting down and looking at a video or photographs of the same campus tour. Even students who partook in a relatively boring tour, walking alone around the interior of a campus building, reported more positive results than those watching a film of that same tour.

There are times in our lives when it makes sense to set ourselves up for success by literally getting fit to do something better. Times when it's really worth paying more attention to exercise and movement, because being in better physical shape will increase our chances of success. Being in better physical shape might help us manage a tricky conversation, for example, or focus for longer on a document, or have more patience. We usually associate wanting to be in better shape with training for a sports event or losing weight or being generally healthier – and that of course makes good sense. But we can also feel the benefits of exercise and movement when we face other challenges. I meet a lot of people who want to be strong and at their best, be it professionally (because of a promotion, a new job, an impending deadline or hitting a new target, say) or personally (recuperating from an illness, moving house, going through divorce or separation, or dealing with ageing parents). At times like these, they want to be at their best, but in my experience, when people take on a new challenge or responsibility there is a tendency to neglect their own physical investment – the things that give them energy.

The Human brain is snapping, *Got to get this done. Got to get this done. What will people think if I don't get this done?*, while the Reptile and Dog brains are getting more and more agitated as they feel neglected. This manifests itself in many different ways. I see people getting caught in inefficient traps – sometimes set by others, sometimes by themselves – 'I'm in back-to-back meetings all day', 'It's always mad at this time of year', 'I'm stupidly busy, no time for lunch' – establishing a belief that the more they work, the more they will get done. Their Reptile and Dog brains will try to interrupt and let people know in other ways – by making them sleepy, snappy or unfocused, for example. There is always a tussle going on between the three brains. When the Dog and Reptile brains are being ignored, they'll escalate their concerns and, after a while, will impose themselves, causing that unreasonable attitude when no food is forthcoming, or that pain if the body has been sedentary for too long, or even illness.

A report in the *International Journal of Workplace Health Management* showed that people who exercise during a work day were 23 per cent more productive than on days when they didn't exercise. Another study, in the journal *Neuropsychobiology*, showed that exercise also slows the brain's mental ageing and can practically buy you back a few years in cognitive health. So perhaps it is time to hunt out your trainers.

What is intriguing is that most of the people I meet can't actually remember making a decision to stop doing the physical activities they enjoy. The activities just began to feature less and less in their lives as other demands intensified and pressures increased. What happened to the importance of being 'properly selfish'?

When I first met Neil, he had recently taken a promotion and now found himself working longer days in an area of the business that needed a great deal of attention. He told me he had always done a lot of exercise, that he had gone running since he was a kid, and now he had let the habit slip. He blamed a hectic work and family life and a need to avoid the traffic and get to work early to make a start on things before his team arrived.

Neil lit up as he spoke about running. Here was an activity he clearly loved which had been part of his routine before the promotion. Now he was choosing to put himself last. And he was noticing a difference in his performance at work. 'It's apparent to me that both age and stress are starting to impact my performance,' he told me. 'I feel like I don't have the energy that I used to throughout the day.' I asked him if he could run once he arrived at work. His immediate response was: 'Well, not for the time I'd like to spend running. Maybe I could manage about thirty minutes tops. I'm not sure it's worth it.' I suggested it might be worth finding out.

The second time I met Neil, he was excited to tell me he had indeed begun running again. The realization of how much it meant to him to run was helping him put himself first. We can all – when we take time to stop and think – choose to put ourselves first in order to be better. 'The best time for me', he said, 'is in the morning. I get up and head out before the rest of the house wakes up, running a minimum of thirty minutes every day. The results have been immediate. I feel happier, more relaxed, less stressed and more in control. I also feel like I have the edge over people because I'm more alert and ready.'

He was enjoying it and commented on the huge difference it had made to his energy levels – and he still achieves what he needs to do. Sometimes more. It is now a few years since he made that decision. When I talk to him about it now, he says his daily running is a priority and dramatically affects his effectiveness. He runs pretty much every day, still for a minimum of thirty minutes. He has made it part of his morning routine, and he makes time wherever he is and whatever he is doing, even on holiday.

There have been times when he hasn't managed to run and, in his words, 'I feel the difference – and so do others in my team. Those days are never as good.'

He has rediscovered the true value of proper selfishness, so he can lead others and himself better.

We can often underestimate the impact we have on others when we choose to look after ourselves. I have one client who now says to her family, 'I'm going for a massage for all of us!'

Neil felt he needed to do a relatively serious form of exercise to make himself feel better. However, you can look after your body energy without taking it to quite this level. Remember the Iowa University research results on the benefits of simply walking? Even something as simple as that can have an enormous effect on helping you feel more in control. Take Alan, for example.

Alan was brought up in a family with a strong work ethic built around doing whatever it takes to get the job done; he also had a strong desire for perfection. He described this to me as 'a dangerous cocktail'. 'It took a very dark moment in my life to change my perspective,' he said, 'a moment when I became so totally overwhelmed through exhaustion that one Monday morning I could not go to work. I had pushed myself so hard there was nothing left to give. It was two months before I was able to return to work.'

Alan was shocked at how he had got to this point without

recognizing what was happening. His professional role entailed finding solutions to problems. Here was one he hadn't seen coming, and now his Reptile brain had solved it for him. I could hear his Human brain trying to find a way through on a completely empty tank. Here, again, was a person neglecting the very things that might provide a useful source of energy, deeming them a distraction.

It was time to pay more respect to his Reptile brain, to create a foundation to help him be more effective in the complicated work he was doing. Mason Currey, in his book *Daily Rituals* (2013), shares the many different and varied ways that artists look after their Reptile and Dog brains: from having naps to eating particular dishes at particular times; from swimming to chopping wood and having regular bedtimes. It was time for Alan to do the same – to provide himself with some body energy so that his Reptile brain could be useful and support his Human brain.

We discussed how Alan could build in some simple ways to manage his energy through regular exercise and re-energize himself throughout the day by taking regular breaks – trying a variety of different activities that he had lost touch with. The key for Alan was discovering the impact of walking. He mentioned that his wife had been talking for a while about getting a dog and that he'd always thought it would be far too much work on top of everything else. Now, however, he thought getting one would help him build a walking habit into his day. Very soon, walking Barney first thing in the morning became an essential part of his routine. The dog and he walked every morning, come rain or shine.

Needless to say he got a lot more physically active. He also began to take his rest, sleep and diet far more seriously. 'I let myself sleep beyond 5 a.m., rest more, stop to eat well rather than on the hoof and, most importantly, make time for my family,' he said. He began rediscovering and reinvesting in his energy-providing moments.

In that 'dark time', weekends had been an opportunity to catch up on work. They had become his survival moments. Now he was clear: surviving was about switching off at weekends – time for him and the family. All of this helped enormously, especially sleeping properly and having intentionally relaxed weekends; however, this was all before returning to work. We knew that, if he was to make a real difference, Alan had to change things there too.

Within six weeks, he was back at work feeling refuelled, re-energized and with a new determination to remain in control. The practice that had the biggest impact, though, was his focus on exercise. As Alan said:

My early dog walk became non-negotiable. It improved my oxygen intake, got my heart pumping and helped clear my head – I could focus more clearly and think through my key priorities for the day. My energy remains throughout the day and, if I ever begin to feel overwhelmed, I leave the office and take a short walk to reinvigorate and think. I feel happier.

Now he even encourages others to walk with him if they want to discuss a project. He also encourages others to have meetings on the move. 'They can often be more efficient when they "walk and talk" – as well as breathing in the fresh air!'

When he has long periods of travel for work – obviously without Barney – he now books a hotel that has a gym, and always sets time aside for an early-morning exercise routine.

So, for Neil it was running for a minimum of thirty minutes every day; for Alan it was walking the dog. Either way, it left them in much better shape to achieve all they wanted. For you it could be anything in between. Or something altogether different and personal.

Here are a few examples of exercise and movement practices that others have tried and say make a difference to their body energy. See if any of them work for you:

_____ Every ninety minutes I go for a walk and get some air.

_____ I make sure I sweat once a day. Get my heart pounding.

_____ I start the day with a five-minute exercise routine and change the routine every week.

_____ Having a dog gives me a reason to walk every day.

_____ I have four stretches that make me feel good and I do them every morning and whenever I need to during the day.

_____ Stairs rather than the lift work for me now.

_____ I always walk up any escalator.

_____ I get off the bus one stop early and walk the last bit through the park.

_____ I try, where possible, to walk and talk with people.

_____ I have stand-up meetings.

_____ I have my meetings on the move.

_____ I keep trainers under my desk so I can run at lunchtime.

_____ I set myself a sponsored goal. This year it was to do a 5k run.

_____ I walk outside whenever I need to recharge my creativity.

 IET

Last but *absolutely not* least, we also need to eat – and eat well.

My husband and I are poles apart in this department. While he finds he cannot think straight if he's hungry, I've had to work hard at making breakfast a priority before starting my day. In the past when I didn't, I would often be ravenous about two hours later, grabbing whatever my hunger demanded from the nearest café and regretting it later.

Thinking about and planning what we eat, and when, can help us perform better. In fact, it can have an impact not just on ourselves but on those who come into contact with us.

One client, Vicky, was very frank on a team day when she revealed how colleagues could get the best from her. She mentioned how aware she was that occasionally she could be unhelpfully grumpy. This was met with a few nods and wry smiles from the team. She went on to explain that it usually had nothing to do with them but had everything to do with the fact she was hungry. It normally happened if a meeting had overrun or was very close to lunchtime and she had failed to bring a snack. In this instance she would become *hangry*. One member of the team piped up, 'Yes – actually we probably recognize the warning signals before you do, Vicky. You either become impatient and snappy or switch off altogether.'

Vicky smiled and shared the fact that her flatmate said the same. She went on to describe how this hangry state felt for her. I noticed that she used words like *taken over* and *compelled* when describing this desire to eat. It became her sole focus. Everything else got in the way. She lost concentration and became very direct, rude even.

Vicky started to manage her hangry state in busy times by eating healthy snacks regularly. She now tries to plan her days around when she can get lunch. She told me,

'When I look at a day of back-to-back meetings, the first thing I assess is whether or not I can escape, just for five minutes, to grab something. If I decide I can't go and get lunch, then I'll ask someone to pick something up for me.'

It is easy for those who don't succumb to hunger like this to perceive her reaction as somewhat extreme, but what and when you eat can have a direct impact on your energy and mental capacity – as anyone who's given a child a packet of Haribo or a Slush Puppy will testify.

On a more serious note, this can have life-changing consequences. Roy Baumeister, a social psychologist in the field of willpower, presents a compelling case from a study his colleagues conducted among some judges in Israel. The results showed that the judges' decisions were directly affected by their diet:

> Parole cases come up in random order throughout the day, but the ones that came up first thing in the morning had a pretty good chance of getting parole, and by the end of the afternoon hardly anybody had a chance of getting parole. It was just a steady downward thing across the day, with two notable exceptions: mid-morning when the judges got a break and a snack – a piece of fruit and a sandwich or something; and then a second break for lunch. At both of those they got more food in, giving them more fuel for glucose. So the chances of getting parole shot up again right after both breaks.

The bottom line is that if anyone who wants parole is offered the chance to have their case squeezed in before lunch, they'd be better off refusing the offer and hanging on till after lunch instead.

It takes energy to make decisions, and our energy runs out. This research suggests that it might be worth paying attention to what and when we eat to give ourselves the best chance to make considered choices about the things that matter to us.

So, if a decision is to be made by you or about you, fingers crossed all parties have eaten.

Here are a few examples of diet practices that others have tried and say make a difference to their body energy. See if any of them work for you:

_____ I always eat breakfast and make sure it includes fruit.

_____ I have a stash of oat cakes and nuts in my drawer.

_____ I know when I am going to take lunch. I actually stop work to enjoy the food away from my desk.

_____ I make sure I have a healthy snack with me all the time.

_____ Smaller portions work for me. I have more energy.

_____ My PA and I have diary rules, like allowing fifteen minutes between meetings to catch my breath and allowing proper time for lunch.

_____ Four of us make sure we all stop for lunch at the
same time and set ourselves little rules, for
example eating out of the building; bringing
an interesting healthy snack; stopping for a
minimum of thirty minutes; no devices.

_____ I have created a food log to track the impact it
has on my energy levels.

_____ I never shop when I'm hungry.

BETTER AT ANYTHING STARTS WITH YOU

Now that you've heard how others have chosen to be more
properly selfish to gain increased energy and clarity, I hope
it might prompt you to try out a few ideas. Just remember
that the secret of body energy is in your S-H-E-D.

Knowing *which* element of your SHED to focus on can
be more of a challenge. The minute one of them is depleted,
it will interfere with the other things you are doing in your
life. Similarly, the moment you pay too much attention to
one, the others will shout. All of them need attention.

When I worked with Annabel, she was trying to choose between two job offers. Her husband had been offered a job abroad, while she had been offered a job in London where they lived. She explained that they were weighing up which would be the better post to accept as a family. She rattled through the situation, speaking very quickly as she didn't have long before she had to hurry home to drive her children to their dance classes. Moving would mean lifting her children out of a routine they were used to. But was it actually better to move now, when they were still young, as they might adjust more quickly? Or should they wait until they were more aware of what was going on? It's a common dilemma for parents.

I asked her how she was doing with her SHED. She retorted, 'Well, I'm off to the gym later. I've been going to the gym as much as I can. I've really been looking after my exercise.' Just listening to her, I could hear how much pressure she was putting herself under. I found myself saying, 'Supposing you didn't go to the gym tonight and went home and relaxed instead. Have a bath?'

Tears welled in her eyes. She paused. 'Yes, I really want to do that. I really want to do nothing – just for a few hours.'

So she did.

Annabel needed her Human brain to be in great shape to help her make the choice that would affect her and her family for the next few years. Her Human brain required the support of her other two brains to do this. She was exhausted, depleted of body energy, and although she had been focusing on exercise as a key part of her SHED routine, it now seemed important to nudge Annabel to pause and pay attention to another part of her SHED.

Annabel decided not to go to the gym and took the pressure off by having a long bath instead. She chose to rest. I'm not saying she had a road-to-Damascus moment in the bath that evening, but pretty soon the family did make their decision. And it was a decision that they were all happy with. They went abroad for three years, the length of her husband's contract, then returned to the UK.

She told me when we met next, 'I was going too fast, and putting "Go to the gym" on my to-do list just added to the pressure rather than reducing it. At that time I actually needed to stop, and choosing to have a bath that night forced me to. *A bath moment* has now become part of our family vocabulary. I say to myself, "This is a bath moment, Annabel. Take it."'

For you, it might be seeing a film, listening to music, meeting a friend, even going for a run. In a world where the hectic pace and constant demands of life seem to have become normal, rest and relaxation have become increasingly sidelined.

One of our team members came up with a phrase at one of our team days which we have all now adopted. When any of us is behaving like their SHED is out of order, whoever spots the telltale signs says, 'SHED off!'

Most of the conversations I have with people aim to

help them identify which aspect to focus on to get their SHED in order so they're in the best possible shape to move in their 'better direction'. Clients are often unintentionally neglecting one aspect and, when I ask them, they usually know which one. Paying a little more attention to one or more aspects of our SHED can help us find new, previously untapped sources of energy.

I'm sure you already know what you could pay more attention to in order to boost your fuel tank. Like any machine, your tank will work at its best if there is the right amount of the right fuel.

Despite clear memories of my father's pre-journey diligence with his car, I confess I have made the mistake of filling my car with diesel instead of unleaded. In fact, it shames me to say I've done it twice. But what struck me (twice) was how quickly the car began to judder, splutter and then grind to a halt. On both occasions I have ended up sitting on the embankment of a busy motorway – as instructed by roadside assistance – waiting and watching as the rest of the traffic (with the correct fuel) goes whizzing past. It's no accident that clients often complain that they're 'running on empty'.

At the same time, when I was on that embankment, I became very aware of the speed, the noise and the pollution that we can get caught up in. When I'm racing along at the same speed, I am blithely ignorant of those details, and assume I will be able to carry on at that pace. The only thing that challenges that assumption is when I put in the wrong petrol or get a puncture. Sitting waiting for assistance reminded me of the value of assisting myself, of looking at the components that we often ignore when we're busy. If we take care of ourselves by paying attention to the basics, we are more likely to have the best possible fuel to move forward. In order to travel towards being better, we need a well-tuned vehicle to get us there.

In my experience, people who immediately commit to trying one thing to help themselves find it makes them feel better and that they can achieve more. And that one practice may be all you need to get your SHED in order.

People I know who perform really well think consciously about their long-term SHED. They take care of themselves, and have developed rhythms and routines throughout the year that mean that, on the whole, they remain in good shape and stay on top of their game. This might include a regular gym class, weekends off or holidays booked in advance.

You may know exactly what it would take to help give you a secure and useful SHED. If so, great, go for it – and let me know what happens. If not, here is a table including all the SHED practices I've mentioned so far.

Sleep/rest	Worth a try?	Impact?
Start going to bed and getting up at the same time every day.		
Set a go-to-bed alarm as well as a get-up alarm.		

99

Make sure you have some 'me time'
in the evening.

Shut down all devices 1 hour before
you go to bed.

If you're lying awake at night,
remember that rest is good too.

Make your bedroom dark, quiet
and cool – a high-quality sleep
environment for high-quality sleep.

Eat supper no later than 2 to 3 hours
before bed.

Limit your caffeine intake during the
day, and avoid it completely for 10
hours before bed.

Take a 20-minute 'smart nap' during
the day.

Create a personal zone in your
workspace for 'me time' so that you
can think, rest or simply create an
energy change.

Put your worries in a bag outside
the bedroom door.

Take a bath.

Banish electronic devices from the
bedroom.

What else could you try?

Hydration	Worth a try?	Impact?
Carry a water bottle – always.		
Make sure there's a jug of water on the table. Finish it by the end of day.		
Allot 3 days a week as caffeine-free and alcohol-free days.		
Set H_2O alarms on your phone for every 2 hours.		
Put a large glass of water by the bed and drink it on waking.		
Limit your caffeine intake during the day.		
Have a non-alcohol drink you love when tempted on one of your alcohol-free days!		
What else could you try?		

Exercise	Worth a try?	Impact?
Go for a walk every day for at least 20 minutes and get some air.		
Make sure you sweat once a day – get your heart pounding.		
Start the day with exercise/ movement.		
Take the stairs rather than the lift.		

	Worth a try?	Impact?
Stretch regularly throughout the day.		
Get off the bus one stop early and walk.		
Walk and talk with people.		
Have stand-up meetings.		
Have meetings on the move.		
Keep exercise shoes in the office.		
Set an exercise goal and get sponsored.		
What else could you try?		

Diet	Worth a try?	Impact?
Always eat breakfast.		
Have a stash of oatcakes and nuts in your drawer.		
Know when to take lunch. Stop to enjoy the food.		
Carry a healthy snack all the time.		
Have smaller portions.		
Create diary rules, e.g. allowing 15 minutes between meetings to catch breath, and allowing proper time for lunch.		

Commit with others to stop and eat together.	

No processed food.

Set up food rules, e.g. never shop when hungry.

Create a food log book.

What else could you try?

I'm not suggesting you try all of these. Or even any of them. But perhaps knowing they helped others construct a strong SHED may nudge you to do something similar.

Below is an example of a client's personal SHED practice that combines all four components:

Sleep/rest	Hydration	Exercise	Diet
Arrive home before 6.30 p.m. at least twice a week	Keep sipping water	Cycle	Cut out the rubbish
	Avoid caffeine during the week	Walk outside daily	Carry a healthy snack
Meditate every other day for 10 minutes first thing in the morning			
Go to bed before 11 p.m.			

If you aren't sure which SHED practices you want to pay more attention to, you could try filling in this next table to understand more about when you are at your best.

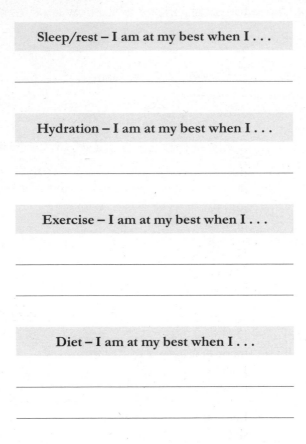

Sleep/rest – I am at my best when I . . .

Hydration – I am at my best when I . . .

Exercise – I am at my best when I . . .

Diet – I am at my best when I . . .

Once you know the sorts of things you want to address, you can assess your progress on your SHED practices by using a table similar to the one below. The examples shared in it belong to one of my clients. The first column is a list of the ingredients that he identified as playing a crucial role in helping him keep his SHED in order. The second column indicates the reason he wobbled and nearly dropped his commitment to the practice. The third column defines the practice he wanted to commit to, and the fourth column records how he is currently doing.

SHED Ingredient	Wobbled because	Resolution	How am I doing?
Take 2 days off each week	Worked 12 days in a row due to unforeseen deadlines	Take weekends off	
Have a reasonable meeting schedule	Had 6 hours of meetings back to back	Instigate breaks and variety	
Limit coffee each day	Drank too many because I had no rest breaks	Max of 2 cups a day before 12 p.m.	
Meditate	Let practice slide	Just do it!	
Exercise	Not enough	Just do it!	
Alcohol	Drank during week	Reinstate weekend-only rule	

And of course, I can't finish this section without catching up on Beverley's story. Remember? We left her with a waterlogged iPad.

She had rung me in tears from her holiday and we arranged to start work as soon as she returned to the UK.

When we sat down and discussed her situation, she cited several episodes at work where she had felt undermined or unprepared.

It was clear to me that, before we could address how she wanted to be should such situations recur, she had to restore her SHED. She had been travelling 200 days a year, giving her all at work, and collapsing exhausted when she got back home, 'loading everything on my poor husband', she said. She wasn't getting a chance to exercise, was attending too many corporate evenings and drinking too much.

She agreed she had to find time to exercise. She had always loved sport and now made no time for it in her life. She had to be properly selfish. She made a commitment to herself to 'sweat once a day'. She became strict with herself and her diary, creating whole days where 'I invest in me. I do yoga and I meditate too.'

As a consequence, she now feels more resilient, more purposeful and much more connected at home. She is able to enjoy herself at work and home. Even though we couldn't save her iPad.

Our Five Energies

Body Energy

Mood Energy

Mind Energy

Purpose Energy

People Energy

5.

CHOOSE YOUR MOOD

'Between stimulus and response, there is a space. In that space lies our freedom and our power to choose our response. In our response lies our growth and our happiness.'

Unattributed, in foreword to Viktor
E. Frankl's Man's Search for Meaning

Just as we have established ways to fuel our body energy, there are some simple ways to help us choose our mood energy too.

Our mood, or emotions, affect what we do on a second-by-second basis and it all happens in a fraction of a second.

OUR DOG BRAIN:

- Is jolted into high alert by the Reptile preparing for a likely friend or foe (instinct).

- Assesses whether it's a likely reward or threat (intuition).

- Ignites conscious emotions, which impel us to move closer or further away.

Our Dog brain helps us to survive. It is constantly working out, from the physical signals received from the Reptile brain, whether something or someone is likely to cause us harm or make us feel great. It does that by creating an intuitive, impulsive response to move us away from or towards something as quickly as possible. Fundamentally, our emotions drive us to movement. It's no surprise that 'motion' sits at the heart of the word. Thousands of years ago, moving was all about survival: moving towards food or away from the predator. Now, in the twenty-first century, things like tricky conversations, high-pressure meetings, exams, facing the boss, or hearing someone shout, spark similar feelings of survival on an unconscious level. We might fall victim to unnecessary nerves, get snappy or over-eager, perhaps shout back, close down or cry. Even though the intent of these emotional responses is always positive, it can result in an unhelpful outcome. By pausing and choosing our mood, we can override our faster, impulsive Dog brain. This pause creates the time for our slower, smarter and more considered Human brain to do what it does best: helping us to devise clever and creative ways to reach the outcome we really want.

A common request I hear is to be better at managing or controlling emotional responses. I work with many men and women who feel they are being 'too emotional' about particular people, decisions or situations and want to manage their emotions so they can move forward. Many find it hard, and sometimes they can't understand why they are not able to exert more self-control.

Few of us are taught how to manage our emotions. Most of us, at some point in our childhood, will have been told to calm down, control ourselves, just relax, or stop how we're behaving. Maybe we've even been told these things as adults. Rarely are we taught *how* to do any of those things. Here's an example from my own life. I was twenty-seven when my father died. My parents were living next to a family who had become great friends. They had a five-year-old son who was very close to my father. He was a kind of grandfather figure to him. They chose not to tell him that my father had died. They felt he was too young to deal with the sadness. On the day of the funeral they kept their curtains closed. They didn't want him to see the hearse pull up outside the house. It was a while ago now but I remember finding this very perplexing. How would he learn to manage his feelings if he was protected from his own or from seeing them in others?

The good news is that there are many examples, including the neurologist and Holocaust survivor Victor Frankl, of people who learn to manage their emotions and choose their moods even when under the most extreme pressure.

Many of us feel that our moods are regularly chosen for us or imposed upon us. It may feel like this is the case, but that is because of our intuitive recollection of previous experiences. Nobel Laureate Herbert A. Simon describes intuition as 'nothing more and nothing less than recognition'. Whether positive or negative, our experiences are filed away by our Dog brain in readiness for any reoccurrences. I am constantly amazed at the power of this sensory filing cabinet to bring past emotional history to bear on seemingly logical decision-makers.

I recall a conversation I had once with a film producer. He told me about a casting session he had had with his boss, the executive producer. They were looking through a pile of audition tapes that actors had sent in. There was one actor that this film producer particularly wanted the executive producer to watch, as he felt he was extremely funny and would be a smart choice. He explained this and put the tape on. His boss happily began to watch, but the film producer noticed her mood change as the tape continued. Sure enough, at the end, she snapped, 'I know he's very funny, but he reminds me of a guy who bullied me at school, so no.' She disregarded the tape without further consideration. Her Reptile and Dog brains immediately connected her to those memories, sensations and feelings. Any considered decision her Human brain might have made was quickly overridden in order to avoid revisiting her unpleasant past experience.

Our senses have an extraordinary ability to bring back

memories and to evoke the emotions we have attached to them. Passing a field of freshly mown grass can propel my husband back to his old school and athletics competitions – he knows this because his heart starts to race just at that familiar smell. A whiff of a particular perfume or aftershave can bring back the memory of someone instantly. Sounds can have the same effect. My mother once fell all the way down our stairs and broke her hip. That sound of her tumbling down our wooden stairs is now so etched on my memory that whenever I hear anyone trip up or down a couple of steps, I irrationally flinch and feel my heart thump – a disproportionate reaction to the situation.

This goes for specific environments too. I have a client whose stomach sinks every time she passes a particular boardroom where she 'chaired a disastrous meeting'. Equally, another client actively returns to a particular room because, when we worked together there, he found a way through a tricky issue. He now takes himself there when he needs to think through challenges, because that room instantly makes him feel more positive. These sensory invitations cause instant reactions in our Reptile and Dog brains and affect our moods – either usefully or not.

CREATE A MOMENT OF CHOICE

We can all find ways to create a moment of choice, a moment when we can actively check our mood and, if necessary, change it. A moment when we are *informed* by what we're feeling rather than *impelled* by it. My clients find it helpful to ask themselves, 'Am I letting my reactions inform or impel me?'

Take Kate, for example.

Kate wanted more choice over how she reacts at home after a long day at work. One day, she'd returned home from work, exhausted, to her six-year-old child. As Kate collapsed in the armchair, her daughter raced over to give her a hug and accidentally knocked a glass of milk flying – all over a brand-new rug.

'I went ballistic, shouting at her for being so careless,' Kate said. 'I demanded that she clear it up before it sank in and ruined the carpet. I know my reaction was disproportional to the incident, but at the time I couldn't stop it.' Her daughter was naturally upset and disappeared to her room in floods of tears.

Kate knew she'd overreacted. 'It felt like a release of all the pent-up emotion of the day,' she said. 'I'm not proud of this at all, but at the time it felt hugely cathartic.' She went straight upstairs and apologized.

For Kate, that moment became pivotal. When we explored it further, she realized she had been working so hard at choosing her mood at work – dealing calmly with high-pressure moments and handling tricky individuals all day long – that she struggled to choose how to respond to this domestic situation with the most important person in her day. She hadn't chosen to react the way she did. She was tired and drained, so her Dog brain found it easier to dictate the response. Its intent was a positive one – to conserve what little energy Kate had left – but consequently it overrode any Human-brain involvement and barked.

Kate's dynamic is a common one. Clients often give themselves completely at work and then collapse at home, with no energy left for their family.

Oliver, a senior executive, got home one night to find his wife waiting excitedly to talk through plans for a future family holiday. Oliver admitted to her that he was completely exhausted after a very trying day at work and asked if they could discuss it another time. She had one more go. He had to insist that he simply couldn't think straight and he needed her to stop so he could relax. She left him alone, only for the quiet to be disrupted by a call on his mobile from the company chairman. He bounded up from the sofa, answered the phone and proceeded to stride around the living room for half an hour in lively conversation with his superior. His wife was quick to point this out afterwards as she dumped the brochure in his lap.

We can all make the effort to choose our moods if we want to – even when we think we're running on empty. If Oliver had spent a bit of time on his way home choosing his mood, he could have bounded in and had a lively conversation with his wife, despite his trying day.

If we want to, we can anticipate and prepare our mood energy in advance of moments that matter to us. It just means we have to pay them a bit more attention and make some deliberate choices about how we feel.

So, what mood do you wish to choose?

Here are the moods that clients find most helpful in maintaining their ability to listen and respond usefully:

- calm

- confident

- positive

- curious

- appreciative

Some of you might read that list and think, *Surely it's useful to show your frustration occasionally*. You wouldn't be alone. Recently a manager said to me, 'I'm sick and tired of having to stay in control all the time. Why can't I get angry if I want to?' and I would say you *can*. But only as long as it's your choice. Unbridled emotions can rarely be trusted – especially when others are around. The impact of an angry word can live long in the memory of family, friends or colleagues.

So, how do you choose your mood? Assuming that your SHED is in good order and you have sufficient body energy, there are five tools that people find useful when choosing their mood: body posture; breath; appreciation; triggers; and self-talk. So, having done your own 'SHED check', you could use any or all of these in the two most common scenarios where paying attention to your mood energy really makes a difference: Before and During.

1. *Before* a moment that matters to you, to help set you up for success and help you stay focused. For example, before:

- arriving home
- a board meeting
- making a complaint
- a presentation
- a tricky conversation
- an interview
- an exam
- delivering bad news
- taking a penalty
- a first-night performance
- a first date
- ending a relationship

2. *During* an emotionally charged situation that you hadn't anticipated, when you sense the first signs of the Reptile and Dog trying to take over. For example, when you:

- receive unexpected results
- are blamed or criticized
- are overtly praised
- are ignored or left out
- bump into an ex
- become lost

- get shouted at
- are caught up in an accident
- are unexpectedly delayed
- are stuck with a needy friend or colleague

In scenarios like these, when we use the five simple techniques – body posture, breath, appreciation, triggers and self-talk – we can choose our mood and maintain the most useful mood energy to support us in getting better.

BODY POSTURE

bored

distracted.

restless

angry.

'You do not run from a bear because you are afraid of it, but rather become afraid of the bear because you run from it.'

William James

When I read the quote above, written by James in 1884, I was curious. Who on earth wouldn't run from a bear if they saw one heading in their direction? What was he talking about?

A few years ago I visited friends in Canada and we stayed in a beautiful region known locally as 'cottage country'. On the fridge was a laminated sign that read: *To anyone thinking of going for a run in these woods – remember: If you see a bear, do NOT run away. Stand your ground and make yourself look as large as you can, stay calm, let them see you and talk to them in a calm voice reminding them you're human and not prey.*

Perhaps Mr James had a point.

The way we use our body can influence not only the behaviour of bears, but also our own ability to maintain a more helpful mood energy. As a teacher I used to reset my energy levels before my next class by shutting the classroom door, jumping up and down, shaking my shoulders out and clapping my hands – a bit like shaking an old-fashioned thermometer to return the mercury to normal. It certainly did the trick, returning me to neutral.

Many clients are surprised at how they can shift their mood if they shift their body first. Whatever is happening in our bodies is important data for our Dog brain. It's looking out for any sign that might mean we are under threat. It conducts a myriad of checks on things like tension levels, heartbeat, temperature, facial expressions, so learning how to use our bodies to choose our mood and therefore conserve our energy is useful.

As a young girl growing up in Cambridge, I would regularly walk through the Backs, where the colleges back on to the River Cam, with my mother. There was a particular part of the river that she loved to take me to so that we could sit and relax. It meant we had to cut across the grass, which wasn't allowed. I remember feeling a mixture of fear and nerves every time we approached the sign saying *Please keep off the grass unless you're a member of the university*. My mother never let this prevent her, though. She would take my hand and say, 'Come on, Sara. Stride across as if you're meant to be here. Smile and walk with confidence, then no one will bat an eyelid.' I remember doing that for the very first time. Striding with confidence – not looking at anyone in case I caught a glimpse of their suspicion. It always worked. We were never stopped. By smiling and striding with intention, I actively replaced the fear and nerves with confidence.

I have followed that mantra a lot since: when I walked home at night as a student; as I walked in for my first job interview; even now, when I walk into a new situation and don't know anyone. In those moments of unease I remember her words: 'Come on, Sara. Stride across as if you're meant to be here.' I now share the same approach with my own children and clients.

It's no surprise that phrases connecting body and emotion pepper our language: *chin up*; *stiff upper lip*; *pick your feet up*; *puff out your chest*; *stand up for yourself*; *pull yourself together*; *grin and bear it*; *get it off your chest*. Our emotions speak through our bodies all the time. When James Joyce wanted to describe the cold, emotionally uncomprehending Mr Duffy in the short story 'A Painful Case', he wrote: 'Mr

Duffy lived a short distance from his body.' It's one of my favourite lines.

I observe many people who appear to live like Mr Duffy. They seem to have cut themselves off from their bodies, from listening to or observing their bodies' reactions. Their heads have turned up to the meeting, but their bodies have just been forgotten.

I attended a workshop several years ago where we took part in an exercise called 'Walking in Others' Shoes'. In it, we went to a park and had to shadow another participant – copy their pace, their stance, stop when they stop, move as they move, all in silence. Then we swapped roles. I was coupled with a man who appeared to be a lot more laid-back than me. The emotional impact our movements had was fascinating. When my partner walked slowly, I did, and as such became more peaceful, more contemplative. When he stopped to look at things, I looked at things. It's true that at first I thought, *OK, OK, it's a duck, come on. Next?* But as time passed I started to enjoy the experience and relax more. When my partner followed me, he said that, while he felt more energized and purposeful, he also felt he had missed a few things on the way . . . and was a bit out of puff! This exercise helped me reconnect with the concept that how I walk – my pace; how I hang my hands; the position of my head; the tension in my shoulders – impacts on how I feel as well as what I see and what I think.

Professor Erik Peper, an expert on holistic health and stress management, has done extensive research on how our body posture can affect our mood. In 2012 he conducted an experiment through which he discovered that, from a helpless, slouched body position, his participants found it easier to recall negative memories and create negative thoughts. Conversely, by taking up a stronger, upright position they found it much easier to recall more positive and empowering ones.

Part of the work I do with clients who want to become better at managing their mood – particularly under pressure – is to help them become more consciously aware of how their bodies respond. I teach them how to be better at observing themselves – at spotting the first physical signs and making deliberate choices about how to respond to them rather than being led by them. I take them through a four-step practice:

1. Become aware of your body signals.

2. Thank them.

3. Deliberately choose your posture.

4. Maintain it.

Let's look at the case of Charles to study this in more detail. Charles was angry about not feeling involved or valued as a member of his company's executive team. Within this group, a handful of key individuals tended to dominate the conversation. In fact they often talked over everyone else and each other. Being a more reflective member of the team, Charles felt irritated by the dominance of a few loud voices. He got on with them all on a one-to-one basis relatively well. But in the executive meetings he was finding them – and his inability to be heard – increasingly frustrating.

'Whenever I feel undervalued or uninvolved,' he told me, 'I just shut myself down, put up a shield and retreat. On the outside I appear quiet and still, but I am boiling up inside. I've always done it. It's my way of dealing with it. Others shout. I shut down.'

It was the way he had always responded to feeling undervalued or excluded, and he wanted to choose a different way of responding. This habit was holding him back. We discussed how it presented itself within his body. He realized the first sign was a tightening of his jaw. This then coursed rapidly through his body, making it rigid and tense.

I asked how he felt in meetings outside the executive team.

'Confident, energized and enjoying it a lot more,' he replied.

'And how do you notice that in your body?'

'I'm looser. And a lot more relaxed. I can feel it here' – he pointed to the middle of his chest – 'like I'm feeling now.'

I shared what else I saw. 'You're leaning in, your shoulders look relaxed and there's a warmth in your eyes.'

I asked him to transfer this looser, more relaxed Charles into the executive meetings. He found it helpful to remember that those signs of tension were his Reptile and Dog brains protecting him. Learning to appreciate their warning signals, and thanking them rather than fighting them, became an important part of his practice – helping him to replace 'shutting down' with 'relaxed and confident'.

So together we evolved a body practice for him to experiment with:

1. Notice when the tension builds in my jaw.

2. Appreciate it.

3. Deliberately soften my jaw, release my shoulders and open my chest.

4. Stay connected, with warm eyes.

'It felt a bit of a battle at first,' Charles said. 'My body was pulling me to shut down against my determined effort to relax the tension. I would imagine a flow of ease running right the way through every muscle – moving my body forward to make myself involved. The more I focused on doing that, the more involved I became. Before I knew it, my voice had followed my body and I was articulating what I wanted rather than being silently irritated.'

Charles now had a practice to counter his own body's reactions – and his mood.

Becoming more aware of what happens to your body under pressure is a great starting point. As a dancer, when I struggled with the flow of moves, my teacher would remind me to find my centre. Once I'd found it, I could balance, turn and transfer my weight quickly and lightly. I felt fully connected, joined up. This in turn made me feel more confident, courageous and optimistic. I still use this invaluable practice when I need to find my own centre and help others build a practice to find theirs.

Mia was another of my clients. She found herself reflecting on her relationship with her mother-in-law, who she found difficult and rude. She had experienced years of hurt and anxiety from their interactions. Every time she tried to explain how she felt, her mother-in-law turned on her – furious that Mia even dared to question her integrity and generosity. Mia and her husband were struggling to figure out how they could make her relationship with her mother-in-law more bearable – something that was particularly important now as they had children. This is how she described to me what happened in those interactions: 'I find myself shrinking and hunching and feeling like I'm six – the same age as my daughter. Before I know it I'm hooked into the emotion of the conversation. Leaning in and getting over-hot. Madly defending.'

Mia wanted more control over her response, to make it more bearable. So her body practice became:

1. Become aware of hunching and shrinking in my back.

2. Appreciate the warning.

3. Connect with every vertebra – pouring strength into each one and pulling my shoulders back.

4. Sit and talk 'as an adult' with strength.

I often find that, somewhere deep in their repertoire,

the people I work with have the posture they need for the particular situation they are in. It's simply a matter of recognizing it, dusting it off and tapping into it.

I met Pat when she came to me in advance of a very important job interview. She'd recently had a spate of them and always came away feeling dissatisfied with her performance – and she hadn't been successful in any of them. When we discussed these experiences, she recognized that her moment of pressure tended to fall in the middle of the interview. She felt confident walking in, was well prepared and, in her words, was 'ready to go'. The point of pressure for her was when the panel asked a challenging question and she felt, in her words, 'very little support coming from across the table'. I asked her to describe what happened to her at that point.

'My stomach turns over and I feel wobbly rather than the confident, secure-in-my-knowledge woman who walked in the door, who knows her stuff and knows she can do the job.'

'I'm sure she does!' I replied. 'And if that confident, secure-in-her-knowledge woman had been asked the question, what would have happened to her?'

Stunningly quickly, Pat answered, 'She would have placed her feet firmly on the floor, sat up straight and said what she knows.' Unthinkingly, she had demonstrated just this posture as she spoke. So where was she feeling the confidence now, I asked her?

She replied, looking down, 'Here in my feet. It's really

helpful when I can feel the floor through the whole soles of both feet. I imagine a firm flow of confidence and data coming up from the floor right to the top of my head.'

What that was doing for Pat was giving her body an immediate sense of stability, helping her connect to herself and return her to neutral.

Pat reported that at that next – very important – interview, as soon as she felt her body start to wobble, she consciously used the practice and placed her feet firmly on the floor. 'I found it strengthened my ability to remain focused on the question rather than my state. The good news is I got the job. The bad news is wearing heels is no longer an option for interviews.' Luckily she wouldn't need to go for another interview for a while.

What Charles, Mia and Pat each now had was a practice that used their bodies to bring their moods back on to an even keel – or neutral, as I call it. Calming, reassuring and aligning their Reptile and Dog brains by deliberately choosing their body posture during an emotionally charged situation.

How might *you* prepare for the most useful mood energy you want by using your body differently?

And how might your body help if you're already in neutral and want to be more proactive?

Alison discovered, through a feedback review, that one of her trusted colleagues considered the area of the business led by Alison to be 'safe, steady and reliable' – rather like 'a familiar cousin'. This infuriated Alison. She wanted her area to be viewed as innovative and risk-taking. She assumed that she herself was coming across as safe, steady and reliable. That also infuriated her. She wanted to change this perception, but wasn't sure how to start.

We discussed how she wanted to be perceived. She told me she wanted to radiate a more dynamic, risk-taking mood. I wondered how she could make some headway through her body, and we began by discussing her exercise regime. She told me she usually started her day by swimming about thirty lengths of breaststroke. I asked her to describe this in more detail. She called it 'a gentle glide through the water'. It was something she enjoyed and, by the end of it, she felt 'refreshed for the day'. To connect her to a more innovative, risk-taking mindset, I asked if there was a different exercise she could embark on that might help that shift. She replied, 'Yes, I could learn to do the crawl. I've never done that.' So Alison set out to learn this more dynamic stroke. One that, in her words, would help her 'cut through the water quicker – with more force'.

She spent the next four months learning this new stroke, and over the course of that time she noticed some interesting by-products:

'I now leave the pool feeling ready to act rather than simply refreshed. I find the metaphor of cutting cleanly through the water really helpful when I want to challenge myself with my thinking and fire the team into action. I had no idea that learning a different physical activity in the pool would have such an impact on how I think and behave out of the pool.'

Another client wanted to find a way to get into

conversations more quickly. Jamie told me he would tend to stay on the sidelines of discussions and meetings, waiting for the appropriate moment to start talking to present itself, and then it would pass and be gone. Or someone else would have said what he wanted to say.

Again, we started with a discussion around his exercise regime. He told me how much he loved playing tennis, especially doubles. He seemed puzzled when I asked him what he liked about playing doubles; he was slightly frustrated that I had gone off the point. As he spoke, however, it became apparent that he much preferred playing from the baseline rather than at the net. He felt he played better when he stayed at the back of the court and waited for the ball to come to him. Together we made the connection that if he were to pay more attention to strengthening his game at the net and interrupting rallies earlier, he might feel better able to take this energy into conversations too. It sounds an incredibly simplistic idea, but that's precisely what he did and the results spoke for themselves.

'It's altered how I sit in the chair,' he told me. 'Actually it's altered how I walk into the room in the first place. I now walk in as if I'm walking from the baseline to the net. I feel my shoulders pull back. I keep my eyes up, as if I'm looking over the net, expecting and looking forward to that ball rather than waiting for it. Obviously no one knows I'm doing this, but it even helps to imagine my racket in my hand.'

A particular change or adjustment within a physical exercise can have an impact on your ability to make progress and be better in another area of your life. A posture choice can bring on a mood choice.

American film director and screenwriter Gina Prince-Bythewood talks similarly about the impact sport had on her confidence:

> When I was little, I was pathologically shy . . . I'm still shy. I'm the woman at a party standing alone in the corner with a beverage in my hand because it gives me something to do . . . How do I walk into meetings with the heads of studios to persuade them to give me millions? . . . Where does my healthy ego come from?
> Sports . . . when you exercise, you become more in tune with your body. You can feel yourself getting stronger. It affects your posture, your gait. You feel like an athlete, a warrior, powerful. That's swagger.

She describes the time she went in to Mike De Luca's office to pitch for *Love & Basketball*:

> I was literally shaking – I'd never directed a film before. Why would he ever give me millions of dollars? . . . I took a deep breath and told myself to just walk into the room like I used to walk onto the court: eyes up, smirk on my face, mad confident in my abilities. I left that meeting with $14 million to make my first film.

For many people, their body posture makes an enormous difference to their mood. The good news is you can choose your mood just by thinking about the exercise.

As Steve Williams told me, when he and his team are waiting in the boat at the start of the Olympic final, they are instructed to 'sit like champions'.

Clients who deliberately use their body as a way of choosing their mood are enjoying the impact. Even something as simple as a smile can help. According to research begun in the 1970s, just making yourself smile can be mood-enhancing.

Recently I worked with some Year 11 students as they prepared for their encroaching GCSE exams. We worked on a number of ways to set them up for success before and during exams. As I'm sure you'll appreciate, getting them to smile while thinking about an impending exam wasn't easy, so I got them to hold a pencil between their teeth so it stretched from ear to ear. This forced them to smile. It encouraged them to feel: *I'm OK. I can do this.*

I have yet to see someone holding a pencil between their teeth in a meeting, but I know that some clients do it just before going in. And one of those teenagers who tried it in the exams told me, 'I thought it was a stupid idea when we practised it. But in the exam I found myself panicking on that last question – and with only ten minutes left. I thought, *What have I got to lose?* I did the pencil thing and it was weird. The panic went away a bit and even the question started to make more sense.' As I said, it seems simplistic, but putting a pencil between your teeth can have a startling effect.

At the other end of the test scale, when Steve Williams was tackling another challenge – climbing Mount Everest – he too mentioned the power of the smile. 'With your fingers going numb and spindrift cutting your face to bits, if you just smile to yourself – and sometimes you really have to force it – you actually start to feel warmer!'

Charles Garfield, who coached the Russian Olympic weightlifting team, noticed that when team members lifted to exhaustion they would grimace – as would we all! He decided to try something. He encouraged the weightlifters, when they got to the point of exhaustion, to smile instead. Smiling enabled them to add two to three more reps to their performance. Grimacing is sensed by our Dog brain as a threat: *I'm not sure I can do this any more*. Smiling reassures our Dog brain so it comes off high alert and, as a result, our performance improves. It makes total sense. It takes effort for our body to contradict our mood and vice versa.

I sometimes speak to people who want to be more open and yet I see them sitting with a rigid and closed body. If you want to be more open and flexible, then start with a more open and flexible body. Try sitting with a furrowed brow and a clenched jaw to ask a genuinely open question. It's tough.

Deliberately choosing your body posture can enable you to choose your mood. It will send signals to your brain, which, in turn, will affect how you feel and, as a consequence, what you do.

So how could you choose a body posture that works for you? To give you some inspiration, here are the ones that my clients tend to use the most:

- Pull your shoulders back.
- Smile.

- Place your feet firmly on the floor.

- Feel the energy from the floor running through to the top of your head.

- Lean towards or away from the person you're talking to.

- Jump up and down/shake your limbs.

And below is a list of some of the more specific body posture practices my clients have found useful to choose their mood.

Body posture practice	Worth a try?	Before?	During?	Impact on my mood?
I smile as I walk into a room.				
I duck into the loo and warm up my face and body. I lightly slap my body from head to toe and end with 4 mini jumps. It picks up my heartbeat and I feel joined up . . . ready to go in.				
I stand or sit as if there is a coat hanger left in my jacket or shirt.				

I close the door and
run round the room,
jumping, skipping.
I have to move to
shake off the old
energy and bring on
the new.

I imagine someone's
grabbed a fistful of
my hair, pulling me
up, making me tall.

When I stand, I
consciously shift my
weight onto the balls
of my feet and off my
heels.

I plant both my feet
firmly on the floor
under the table to
feel rooted and solid.

I sit so I can feel the
small of my back
against the chair. It
reminds me to listen
more.

When I want to
contribute more,
I purposefully lean
in and connect with
my eyes, so I can't
retreat.

When I feel myself
getting irritated, I
look up and take a
moment to see the
whole room and
everyone in it. It
helps me connect to
the wider vision and
literally gives me a
bigger picture.

I lean back and
imagine my
shoulders touching
behind me.

I had a habit of
banging the table
when I felt strongly
about something, so
now I shake my
hands out before any
interaction and
gently hold them
together in my lap.

I regularly steal from
my dance training
and imagine a thread
running through
me – out the top of
my head and down
through the floor. It
keeps me balanced,
centred and in
control.

When I'm turning
something over and
over in my mind,
getting nowhere,
I step away from my
chair. I feel instant
relief as I leave the
thought behind on the
chair. When I look
back at the issue from
afar I feel more
hopeful and start to
see options.

I walk listening to a
piece of music I love
with a strong
rhythm. I walk to
that rhythm –
stepping strongly
on the beat.

What's yours?

BREATH

'All human energy is breath. The body houses you and the breath powers you'

Patsy Rodenburg

Most of us take our breath for granted. Thankfully, it's one of those basic needs that our Reptile brain takes care of, and it doesn't require any conscious effort from us. However, using it more consciously can provide the handrail we need when we're choosing our mood. It's a powerful resource, it's available at any time and it costs nothing. A lot of people I meet, once introduced to the power of breath, continue to use it, either as a way of setting themselves up for success in a pre-performance routine, or as a way of stabilizing themselves in a moment of pressure. When I was learning the violin as a child, I was taught to manage my nerves through my breathing. Now, whenever the similar bodily sensations of fear and pressure make themselves known, this breathing practice kicks in automatically.

I built upon this habit – courtesy of NCT tuition – to help me through two births as well. In fact, my 'birth breathing' has become a source of hilarity for my family. We visited Thorpe Park for my son's thirteenth birthday and – so as not to look a complete wimp – I queued up for a ride that by all accounts was 'exhilarating and fun'. Frankly it was neither. Being turned upside down over and over again with only a flimsy belt between me and the ground was in no way exhilarating and certainly not fun. In my 'perfect-moment photo', when the park's camera flashed, capturing the family for posterity, the children were wide-eyed and screaming with delight. I was in a state of deep concentration, eyes clamped shut, lips pursed, caught in the middle of a looooong exhalation. Still, it got me through. It gets me through visits to the dentist too. All thanks to Mr Bass, my violin teacher.

Body and oxygen are interdependent. When we work with our breath, we are working with the body too.

Take Harriet, for example.

A senior leader in a multinational corporation, Harriet had asked me to work with her on her conference speech. There was nothing unusual about that request, and I turned up to help her do just that. She then launched into a long tale about the previous year's event where she had fainted in front of about 700 people and was carried off stage by her colleagues. What was intriguing was that, as she described this episode, she kept repeating, 'I don't know what happened because I wasn't remotely nervous.' On further enquiry, it became evident that she'd been so busy preparing her slides that she really hadn't had any time to prepare herself. 'But that was OK,' she said, 'none of us had. We were all up against it.'

She'd been sitting on the front row as the conference opened, knowing she was underprepared. 'I watched them walk up, hold their own, do a great job and then it was my turn. I got up, walked on to the stage and put my notes on the podium. I remember feeling a bit odd and then . . . I was at the side of the stage on a chair.'

I realized that for Harriet to accept that she was

nervous and thank her Reptile and Dog brains for the warning was a step too far at this point. Here was a woman who had chosen to ignore the warnings and had literally been taken out of the situation to protect her from what the brains had perceived to be possible humiliation. My job was to help her feel confident to walk back on that same stage, ten months on, in front of pretty much the same people, deliver a great presentation and stay upright.

Between us, we created a pre-performance routine that included a breathing technique for her to call on when she needed to maintain a calm energy. Harriet had believed that all she needed to do was prepare her slides. That's a common belief with busy people: *I know what I am going to say. It's all here in my slides.* She hadn't, however, paid any attention to preparing herself.

As we worked on preparing her for the next conference, it became more and more evident that sitting on the front row waiting for her turn hadn't helped. 'I could only see this huge expanse of stage. I think that's where it began. The self-doubt kicked in and got louder in my head. In fact, just thinking about it now makes my heart race.' She was beginning to accept that perhaps her nerves had played a part, and we could now start to develop a practice. The first thing I did was encourage Harriet to watch and feel her breath.

I used to love watching my children sleep as babies. When you watch babies sleep, their breath drops deep into their bellies, rising and falling effortlessly – smoothly and deeply. As adults, the way we breathe changes, particularly when we feel under pressure. We tend to snatch short, shallow breaths. When we do this we limit the amount of oxygen we supply to our body, and then we can't function at optimum capacity. As a result, our ability to use the Human brain is hindered. That can make it harder to come up with ideas, connect with people, listen or stay focused. When we really pay attention to our breathing, we are likely to have more energy and feel more in control – to choose our mood. When I ask clients to do this and then to inhale, they often take a deep breath and hold it in their neck and shoulders. This is actually restrictive. It seems counter-intuitive to take the breath down into our stomach, but that is what I ask them to do.

So I asked Harriet to place one hand on her chest and the other on her stomach. I asked her to breathe in and say which hand moved more when she did. She confidently told me, 'The top hand – the one on my chest.' A great deal of our time together was spent helping her connect to her breath and move it lower in her body.

I asked her to try actively using the next inhalation to move her bottom hand – visualizing the breath dropping low into her body – while keeping the breath smooth and continuous. The gentle pace is very important.

There is a wonderful stillness that happens at the end of both an inhalation and an exhalation. A small beat before our body impels us to continue. I find the stillness in that beat hugely calming, and I encourage many of my clients to connect with that natural beat too – as a point of reconnection to themselves. Patsy Rodenburg, the world-renowned voice coach, who I once had the privilege of working with, calls it 'a fraction of a second when the body feels suspended and ready'. I have clients who practise connecting to that beat to help them choose their mood.

Harriet spent time repeatedly practising this rhythm. In through the nose for a count of three and out through the mouth for a count of seven, noticing where the breath went in her body; visualizing it expanding the lower body. As Harriet felt more familiar with the rhythm – making it as smooth and continuous as possible – she practised it standing, sitting and lying down. She was building the confidence to do it anywhere, any time, under any pressure. It was entirely portable.

When it came to the actual day of the conference, Harriet stood at the back of the room – early – giving her the opportunity to watch people arrive, to actually see her audience this time. Playing through her headphones was a piece of music that she had been using to breathe to. The rhythm helped her keep her breath continuous and smooth. When it was her turn to go on, she went striding through the audience – or, as she put it, 'tom-catting my space'. She stood on that stage, without a podium, and began: 'Now, those of you who were here last year, you can relax. I'm going to remain standing this time.'

And she did. The practice had paid off. This is what Harriet said about that process:

I'd been surprised by my body. And I really did not want it to happen again. Working deliberately with my breath meant I had to pay attention to it until it became more natural and habitual. That took effort. I set my phone to remind me to do the deep-breathing practice four times a day. Increasingly I found focusing on a slow out-breath really helped me. First I did it on my own, very obviously, and then I tried it more subtly, in meetings – privately focusing on a smooth, continuous out-breath. It would instantly allow me to feel calmer. I grew to really enjoy that moment of pause at the end of a breath, and have suggested it to my son when he plays cricket before he goes out to bat.

When you mention using your breath to people it can provoke some interesting reactions. Some absolutely understand the importance of using it well to complete a race, play the saxophone, sing, meditate or enhance their yoga experience. However, when it comes to thinking about using it more deliberately to remain calm during a tricky personal conversation, or in an exam, a meeting or a presentation, some are less than convinced. It's as if it is viewed as a fluffy 'nice-to-have' rather than a vital ingredient.

My business partner tells a great story by way of demonstration:

In a high-stress situation, working as a Marine with American forces, we were all invited to a session called 'Breathing'. Many of us didn't see the point and declined the invitation. Six weeks later, another invitation arrived from the same teacher. This time the session was called 'Combat Breathing'. Naturally, we all accepted. After that one session we felt real benefits, feeling calmer and more in control, so more able to be effective. As a result we readily committed to being drilled in slower diaphragmatic breathing as a key technique for preparing for, performing and recovering from high-pressure situations. We were all taught the same drill but encouraged to adapt it for ourselves, as long as we kept to six breaths or fewer per minute.*

In US Navy SEAL training, all recruits are now drilled in 'Arousal Control' – a simple breathing technique to help them better manage their fear responses during their toughest challenges. But why is focusing on a slow exhalation so helpful in calming us down?

When we decide to breathe out slowly in what could be a moment of pressure, it prompts our Dog and Reptile brains to say, *Hang on a minute, this can't be that bad if they have time to take a long and steady breath out. If they were really in danger, they wouldn't be doing that.* It tricks them into allowing our Human brain a moment of choice. This is an oversimplification of what happens, but many clients find it useful enough to start taking their breath seriously.

The business consultant Greg McKeown, who has worked with Bill Rielly, Head of Partner Marketing at Apple, for many years, wrote in the *Harvard Business Review*

* On average, a person at rest takes sixteen breaths per minute.

that paying attention to his breathing helped Bill reduce his level of stress. Bill started small, by taking three deep breaths each time he sat down at his desk. He found it helped him relax. After three breaths had become a habit, he decided to breathe deeply for a few minutes a day, and found he was more patient, calmer and more present. Now he does it for thirty minutes every day. It restores his perspective while enabling him to take a fresh look at a question or problem and come up with new solutions.

Steady breathing means a steady mood. Under extreme emotional stress, though, this can be hard, as we'll see below.

MANAGING MY FUR-BALL FURY

Ben was due in court. He was in the middle of a hugely acrimonious divorce. He came to me because he wanted help articulating himself much more calmly in the next hearing. He had been told that he was too emotional and as a result was losing his clarity and credibility.

Ben was angry. With his wife, with himself and for his children. The more he talked about the divorce, the more furious he became. His words tumbled out at a chaotic speed, and he became redder, hotter and less coherent. I was finding it hard to listen to the facts because his emotions were screaming much more loudly.

'I feel like the anger is literally stuck in the back of my throat and I want to cough it up,' he said. 'It's like a fur ball of fury and I struggle to speak in the way I need to speak to be listened to. I also find it so difficult to look at her in the court. Seeing her enflames the fury. I have to find a way of controlling the emotion.'

I helped Ben to focus on his breathing.

He had to learn to breathe out. It sounded like all he was doing in those high-pressure moments was gulping air, bracing himself, holding everything he felt so strongly about in the back of his neck. I asked him to focus on taking a few seconds to pause and breathe well before speaking. This would buy him time to manage his feelings. To choose his mood.

We agreed that drilling this as a discipline was the only way it would work.

We practised together. I would throw questions at him; he would focus on his breath (three beats in, seven out). It had to be purposefully long and slow at first. He hated that: the pause felt like an eternity to him and he felt he looked 'clueless'. To me, though, it looked like he was in control, thoughtful and deliberate. With practice, he managed to reduce the length of the pause and still connect to the breathing pattern.

The next time he had to attend the hearing, he put this new skill into practice. Unfortunately, he did not get the result he wanted. However, after having been formally reprimanded in the last hearing, the judge now took the time to commend him on the way he had managed himself.

My yoga teacher has a great phrase when she talks about

breathing out. She says, 'Empty yourself.' Ben had learnt to empty himself by using his breath in order to let him choose how he used his words.

Breathing is also often overlooked when we deal with other sorts of communication, for example writing or reading emails. Recently a client told me he decided to take three deep breaths and pull his shoulders back before opening his emails first thing in the morning. Why? Because the week before he had sent me this:

> Help! I found myself slamming out a long email to my boss describing my disappointment. I told her just how I felt: really let down. How her decision seemed like a personal attack on all the work my team and I had been focusing on over the last two months. Did she not fully understand what we were trying to achieve?
>
> Whilst it felt good to write at the time, the repercussions of sending this have wasted about five hours of valuable time this week in conversations to repair the damage. Shouldn't have sent it. Need to work on a more effective strategy!

Our breath can be instrumental in helping us to choose our mood. I hear from clients on a regular basis telling me how, when they pay more deliberate attention to their breath – getting more oxygen into them – they can press Pause and achieve a breakthrough moment.

Here are the two most common ways that clients use their breath to help them choose their mood:

1. To be calmer

Slow exhalation (three beats in through the nose then seven beats out through the mouth). Place hands on stomach to check that it expands on the inhalation and contracts on the exhalation.

2. To be more alert

Pant in and out through the mouth five times. Sometimes it is helpful to imagine you have five candles in front of you, and you are quickly going down the line, blowing them out. Repeat if necessary (probably best done in private).

Below is a list of some of the more specific breath practices that individual clients have found useful when choosing their mood.

Breathing Practice	Worth a try?	Before?	During?	Impact on my mood?
Before a tricky meeting, I place both hands on my stomach, inhale through my nose and, without raising my shoulders, connect with the pause moment at the top of the breath, remind myself what I want to achieve and then let it out. This gets me poised for action.				

I have a certain picture
I focus on. It's above
eye level, making me
lift my head slightly.
I consciously breathe out
to that point for a count
of 7. It reminds me to
let go of the detail.

When I feel myself
getting angry in
company, I focus on my
breathing. I connect the
anger to my breath and
breathe it out. This
helps me start again.

If it's near the end of
the day and I need to
keep going, I'll find a
place – somewhere
private – and pant: in
through my nose, out
through my mouth.

I now make 'breath
breaks': I close my eyes
and just focus on
breathing in for a count
of 3 and out for a count
of 7. I do that 3
times – it connects me
with me.

To halt my Gut-to-Gob moment, I take a deep breath and let it support my thought – I then let the out-breath be the impetus for the statement. It slows me down.

Before I go into a space to present, I stand in the room on my own and 'breathe the space' – imagining my breath touching all the corners of the room. I then believe I can reach the audience too.

Before I open my emails, I set my state by taking 3 smooth, deep breaths. It allows me to read and get through them calmly.

When I breathe out slowly I feel more powerful. It allows me to regain control over my reaction.

I walk away, then take 2 focused inhalations and exhalations. This helps me reset.

What's yours?

Let's pause for a moment.

Left to their own devices, our three brains will often end up deciding on well-intentioned but unhelpful moods.

Deliberately choosing our posture and breath helps us slow the brains down – returning us to neutral.

This gives our Human brain the chance to decide on the best course of action.

The following three ingredients can help us choose and sustain the most healthy and helpful mood:

Appreciation

Triggers

Self-talk

'Find the good. It's all around you. Find it,
showcase it and you'll start believing in it.'

Jesse Owens

When I think back to all those years walking into my ballet school, one thing strikes me. As soon as I walked into
the building I could see evidence of success – a trophy
cabinet, and pictures of dancers from the school who had
recently won awards or gained an extra grade. Theatre
foyers are often peppered with framed photographs of
successful past shows, many of them signed by the actors
involved. And there are certain companies whose recep-
tions I love walking into because I get an immediate sense
of the pride they have in their products, and the impact
they have had on their area of business. It genuinely shifts
my mood – and I haven't even contributed to these

achievements. I immediately feel more enthusiastic about working with them.

So what about *personal* trophy cabinets? Sometimes I stand in front of groups of clients and ask, 'How many of you could bring to mind right now a story of something you've done that's made you feel proud?' Very few hands tend to go up. When I then ask, 'How many of you have a story where you've messed up?' the hands fly up. We seem to recall those more negative moments much more easily.

We cannot outperform whatever we think of ourselves. So it is vital that we have the best version of ourselves to hand to connect to when we need it.

How do you connect to you at your best?

In his book *Bounce* (2010), Matthew Syed, a former Olympic table-tennis player, shares how he did it before a match. He describes how, after completing a rehearsed sequence of deep-breathing exercises, he would bring to mind one of the most inspiring table-tennis matches he ever played in, using all his senses to connect him to his best:

> Seeing the wonderful strokes, applauding the audacious attacks . . . feeling the sensuousness of the ball on the paddle, the uninhibited flow of my movement and the exhilaration of the playing to the best of my ability . . . sensing a deep and growing feeling of optimism.

The high level of sensory detail in his practice is interesting and is the key to the strength of his connection. In my experience, the more detailed the client's recollection of their achievement, the better. Syed goes on: 'I can feel my confidence solidifying. I can feel the doubts dissolving. I am feeling better and better.'

Now of course, unlike Olympians, we mere mortals have a much harder task on our hands. We're not trying to get better at one discipline. We are normally faced with an array of different challenges. So, to boost ourselves, we have to try to draw on a number of different trophies in our cabinet – times when we were at our best. As I mentioned above, it helps if we make those trophies as detailed and memorable as we can.

Jo had worked in one organization for most of his working life and was incredibly reliable. He was excellent with detail, super-organized and always got a kick from delivering to a deadline. However, Jo now had a different challenge: for the first time he had been asked to lead a team for a project, one that would be instrumental in delivering the commercial target the organization was after. It would mean Jo attending different meetings and regularly giving updates on team progress. While he felt privileged to have been asked, he also felt somewhat alarmed by a sudden lack of confidence.

When we met, one of the key things that made a difference for Jo was spending some time reflecting on his past achievements and appreciating what he had done to make them happen. As I prodded him to tell me more about them, and which skills/strengths he had brought to each, they started to became more colourful, more textured with detail, and so more helpful to both of us in appreciating the part he had played. However, when I asked him how he connected to those achievements now, he said, 'Well, I don't.'

One of the more detailed trophy moments Jo described was the time he'd spent as the coach of his son's football team. He told me about their league statistics; his belief in every one of the boys, irrespective of their ability; the fun training exercises he had put them through and the improvement they had demonstrated over the year. Most important of all was the pride his son had shown when he had said, 'My dad's the coach.' We agreed that this was the one proud story that could hold some clues about how to approach this new challenge he faced as a manager.

The next time Jo and I met in his office, he proudly gestured to his wall. Beside his computer was his emerging 'trophy cabinet': pictures of the team, newspaper cuttings and a photograph of him with his son.

'Having to bring them to the front of my mind felt very awkward at first,' he said. 'Uncomfortable even. I was thinking, *Why on earth are you making me do this fluffy nonsense, focusing on my past achievements? I have real business issues to deal with, for God's sake, and I need help addressing those.* It's already been far more useful than I thought. I surprised myself with the trophies I remembered. Seeing them every day makes me feel good. It's uplifting to see what I've done, and it helps to connect to those trophies when I'm feeling the pressure. It's simple and surprisingly helpful.'

Jo made good use of his trophy cabinet to power himself up. He now appreciated the strengths and skills he had shown as a football coach, and was therefore able to increase his confidence at work.

By contrast, when I met Alexandra, she was ready to quit her professional life:

> I've made a decision that the boss doesn't rate me. I find myself acting differently. I'm quieter in meetings. I sit back. I'm as strong as ever with my team but he gets under my skin. I know I'm switching off, disconnecting, but I feel I can't do anything about it and I hate that. I don't just want to survive, I want to thrive and push forward – but I don't know how. It feels personal. His opinion is starting to invade my every waking thought. I'm bringing work home, and not real work, not real issues that can be solved around the dinner table, personal issues that are impacting my confidence and self-esteem. Even my children know his name. It isn't good for any of us.

Alexandra had clearly been thrown off-course and used words like *rocked* and *unresourced* to describe how she felt. I asked about her past achievements, and it transpired that Alexandra – who by her own admission had been very successful – was choosing to ignore all her successes in the company. 'I've packed them away.' she said. 'They don't feel relevant to the current situation. They were from a different era.'

I asked her to unpack them, to revisit them. How did that make her feel?

'Just reading the thank-you notes people had sent me, looking at the comments and the successes, was brilliant. It reminded me that they were me. They were my DNA. It gave me an unexpected boost and a renewed sense of hope.'

I often witness clients ignoring the resources they have available to them, as they recount moments when they wish they had said this or hadn't done that. It's as if they have completely lost sight of the times when they have been resourceful before. Appreciating our successes – being specific about the strengths that enabled us to achieve them – fires up our confidence and helps shift our mood energy.

Alexandra's success stories belonged in her trophy cabinet, where they could be regularly revisited.

'I made a trophy wall of my own,' she said. 'I made time to relive and reread my trophy wall ahead of meetings, to prove to me (and to others) that I was in the race.'

Connecting to our achievements from the past really can help us to achieve in the present. When clients are encouraged not only to recall a proud moment in their past but also to truly appreciate it, to shine a torch on it, and notice and bank what they did in that moment, I often see a shift. It's as if I can hear the Dog brain say, *Ahhh, OK. I remember now. You're more than able to deal with this. I can relax. I'll stand aside and let the Human brain take control.*

Clients who create and regularly refresh their own trophy cabinets find them an excellent source of mood energy. They do this in many different ways. Here is one example:

> I write them down. I have a folder in my inbox called 'Thank Yous' and I keep them there. I look at them when I need a boost. I take time to recognize what I'm being thanked for. I acknowledge it and recognize that I own it. I bank my strengths to give me strength. There's one in particular I connect to when I'm under pressure.

I encourage my children to create theirs too, in whatever way they like. My son has carved three marks in his shelf (not really what I had in mind) that continually remind him of key achievements he's proud of. My daughter creates hers pictorially, usually on her phone. *Put that one in your trophy cabinet* has become part of our family vocabulary.

If we aren't in the habit of deliberately recalling our trophies, it's much harder to do so in a moment of pressure – when our Dog brain is impelling us to bark, cower or wag. It's worth knowing which trophy moment provides you with the most useful mood energy before the pressure moment. Be deliberate about it. Have fun with it. Make it as vivid and specific as possible. No one else need know – just you. Pull confidence from your past to choose your mood in your present.

To give you some ideas, here are the most common themes that people seem to draw confidence from:

- A meaningful personal relationship.

- Staying connected to a personal value.

- An educational or sporting achievement.

- A promotion.

And below is a list of some of the personal trophies that clients use to choose their mood:

- My first-class degree.

- Climbing to base camp and getting down again without extreme altitude sickness.

- Looking after my mother when she was diagnosed with cancer.

- Completing my first marathon.

- Passing my GCSE Maths aged twenty-four.

- Giving birth without pain relief.

- Successfully working and bringing up two small children on my own.

- Giving up my job and deciding to travel.

- Leaving my husband.

- Leaving my job to be with my son in America.

- Learning to swim at the age of forty-seven.

- Learning Japanese.

Trophies can be displayed in many ways, but here are the most common methods that people use:

- A personal scrapbook
- A desktop file entitled 'ME'
- Items pinned on the wall
- A 'yay moments' box or drawer

My invitation to you now is to pick up a pencil and write down, on a piece of paper, in the margins of this page perhaps, or even in your own 'yay moments' book, the stories that you are most proud of. As you've seen from the list above, they can be as small or as big as you like – as long as they make you feel positive and give you confidence about being you. Write them down. Give them titles. And try to include whatever details you can remember about each one – feelings, comments and images. Try to bring colour to as many of them as possible. Then, just as Jo did, you can pull the one to the front of your trophy cabinet that gives you the confidence you need for your next challenge. Build your own trophy cabinet, bulging with facts, figures and memories.

Below I have compiled a list of some of the personal trophy cabinets that clients use to choose their mood:

Trophy cabinet	Worth a try?	Before?	During?	Impact on my mood?
I email myself on a Friday with all my proud moments from the week.				
I've built my own collage of photos, memories of my proud stories.				
When I go home in the car I say my proud moments out loud to myself.				
Before every board meeting I make time to connect with my 'proud wall'.				
On my screensaver I've created a Gratitude Page that I look at every day.				
I've made a trophy wall. I make time to relive and reread my trophies.				
Every time I have a 'yay moment', I write it down in my 'yay moments' book, which goes everywhere with me. These moments can be small or large, but they are a source of energy to help me keep going.				

I felt like I was unable to
make progress without a
metaphorical hug. I now
provide myself with a
'hug' when I need it by
connecting to a specific
proud story and
appreciating the part I
played in it.

Before every audition or
meeting I make myself a
cup of tea, sit down for 5
minutes and watch my
showreel to remind
myself of how much I've
achieved.

What's yours?

Now you're ready to move on to . . .

Triggers are powerful. They affect us in an instant, particularly the negative ones. *When I hear that voice, it sets my teeth on edge*; *That look makes me want to . . .*; *I just have to see that sign and I . . .*; *What really presses my buttons is when . . .*

But there can be just as much power in a *positive* trigger. Resilient people are really good at tapping into that power for their benefit. And using positive triggers is something that we can all learn to do.

I have a silver meditation ring that I bought while on holiday in Canada. Subtly engraved across the top of it is the phrase *Everything you need is within*. I only have to touch it – turning it on my finger, calling to mind what it says – to trigger in me a feeling of calm confidence, so that I can continue, whatever the challenge.

While the ring isn't attached to a specific trophy moment or experience from my past, it is a 'quick start' trigger, a reminder to appreciate myself and all that I carry 'within'.

A trigger acts as a spark, a short cut if you like, to help reconnect your senses to how you've been in the past and how you want to be in any particular moment.

Remember when Harriet was about to speak at the conference? As she stood breathing at the back of the conference room, she was listening to her favourite tracks on her headphones. That helped her connect to the Harriet who danced, felt free and relaxed. That made her smile. Music is a powerful trigger because it activates so many of our senses.

People I work with often have a lot of fun finding the perfect trigger to help them choose their mood. Sometimes they discover more than one.

One man I worked with had a picture rail in his office and, over the years, he gathered on it a variety of triggers that made him feel good, including a threepenny-bit coin his mum had given him; a thank-you card he'd been sent; and a ticket from a concert of his favourite composer's work. They represented and connected him to moments and moods in his life that he really appreciated. You could walk into his office and not even notice them.

He described what he did in moments of pressure: 'I walk into my office, shut the door, look at my picture rail and breathe them in, taking a moment to fully appreciate each one and what they mean to me. I drink them in. It helps me reboot. I then swiftly walk out again, feeling a lot more energized and in control.'

A client who was a barrister kept a pebble in his pocket. He'd taken this pebble from a beach he loved. He used to spend hours walking and sitting on this beach, and it represented calm relaxation. The beach – for him – was a place of possibility. He'd found creative solutions while walking on that beach. Holding the pebble was a quick, tangible way for him to connect to that feeling – a resource he knew he had but sometimes felt unable to access, particularly in court.

For me, a story that really encapsulates the power of a trigger, though, is this one from my son. He was about to embark on his first big role in a TV series and was excited about the project: a drama about hospital patients, inspired by real events and real people. It was based on a book written by one of the patients, Albert, about his life as a child in the hospital. He had spent a decade with cancer living there. My son was to portray him and was eager to find a solid connection with the man behind the character. As part of the preparation, they met several times. Albert spoke about the absence of his parents in hospital. He described how, because they had been unable to visit often, he sought parental figures within the hospital, and felt he had both real parents and hospital parents. Occasionally the hospital parents were nurses or doctors, but most of the time they were older patients who had experienced more of life, travelled to places and had relationships. They'd done things he hadn't. Just before filming started, Albert told my son this story:

One night, my favourite older patient crossed the ward and woke me up. He handed me a poker chip from a Venice casino. He died shortly after, but the chip constantly reminded me of the outside, real world, pushing me to get better. The idea that I might, one day, be able to go to Venice and use this chip filled me with hope that leaving the hospital was imminent.

At this moment in his story he reached into his pocket, pulled out that same poker chip and handed it to my son, saying, 'For you.'

My son carried this chip in his pocket as a trigger to connect to the mood energy he needed for the work. It was a physical, personal connection to Albert himself, above and beyond the lines.

Scientific research has shown that the stronger the original emotional state associated with the trigger, the stronger the emotional response will be whenever the same trigger is encountered in future.

It doesn't matter what your trigger is. What matters is that it works for you.

A few years ago I saw the athlete Michael Johnson being interviewed by Matthew Syed. Johnson spoke about how he had received a letter from Ruth Owens, widow of Jesse Owens, praising him as the runner who most reminded her of her late husband. Jesse Owens was Johnson's hero. Jesse's drive and determination had inspired Johnson to be a better athlete. This letter became his pre-race trigger.

Actually we see triggers across the board in sport. They are almost the norm, even at the highest level. A good example is the All Blacks rugby team, who have used triggers to create a more useful mood when performing under match pressure. With help from forensic psychiatrist Ceri Evans, who explained to the All Blacks what the brain does under pressure, they established two states: 'Red

Head' (Reptile and Dog), the unresourceful state in which you are off task, panicked and ineffective; and 'Blue Head' (Human), the optimal state – when you're on task and performing to your best ability. The players began using individual triggers to switch from Red to Blue. Richie McCaw would stamp his feet, literally grounding himself, while Kieran Read would stare at the furthest point of the stadium, searching for the bigger picture.

However, while the power of a trigger is openly accepted in the world of sport, it seems to be less commonplace in business and general life. I think it's worth nicking. Clients of mine who deliberately choose and connect to a trigger, or triggers, say it helps them to pause and shift out of an unhelpful mood into a better one.

Colin had a reputation for being 'volatile but smart'. He spent a lot of time negotiating with clients either on the phone or in meetings. We began working together because he wanted to lose the 'volatile' tag – and yet he also rather liked it. He felt it meant that 'people didn't try to get away with things'. When I talked to him, it seemed as if his life was increasingly full of negotiation. He was a single parent and was the main carer for his mother. He was quite a private man, so no one at work knew much about his circumstances.

We talked about how difficult he found it to remain calm. He got easily frustrated with processes and people slowing things down – unnecessarily in his view. His default was to snap. I asked if there was a time he could recall when he hadn't snapped at work.

There was: a conversation where he'd managed himself 'surprisingly well':

> I was in the back of a cab and had to take a call with someone from my team. It was going to be a difficult conversation and, for whatever reason —that I just haven't been able to pin down — I handled it remarkably well. I listened, stayed calm and curious, articulated my frustrations and the call went much better than I had expected.

As we parted company, I suggested that he might want to think of something physical that could act as a trigger to connect him to the energy he had found during that phone call.

At our next session, there it was on his desk, right next to the phone: a model of a black cab. On the bonnet he had painted (with Tippex) the initials *SC*. He smiled and said, 'I only have to catch sight of it and it helps me reconnect to how I *stayed calm* in that conversation.'

The black cab and its large initials became a constant reminder of that specific taxi ride where he had found that useful mood. The more distinctive the trigger, the stronger the power of the trigger to take you back to that particular moment.

Another client, Anne, used something from her own business to come up with her trigger. With a background in manufacturing, Anne understood how anyone has the potential to stop the production line to correct a possible fault – saving significant rework costs. 'Rework' is a big idea that she picked up from her time in Japan. A lot of time can be wasted correcting things after products have been poorly produced, so it's much better to stop and fix the problem, even though that can feel slower at the time. In one of Anne's factories, the line was therefore halted if you pressed a big red Stop button. She loved that concept.

A highly regarded CEO, Anne cared passionately about her businesses and particularly her teams. Being this passionate, she knew that she sometimes acted too impulsively and – although well intentioned – the rework cost could be considerable. Before a likely impulsive reaction, she decided to conjure up an imaginary big red Stop button. She has even put a picture of one in her office, though no one understands its significance.

Connecting to my Stop button allows me a moment of pause before reacting. I find I can then consider and check my intentions and the possible consequences of my impulsive behaviour and reactions. The Stop button reminds me to go slow to produce a better result.

A trigger can reconnect you with how you were when you were at your best.

From the proud stories now in your trophy cabinet (see 'Appreciation'), pick a distinctive trigger (or two) to help you connect to them and choose your mood when you need it.

Here are the most common examples of useful triggers.

- A picture on your phone
- Music
- A piece of jewellery
- A repeatable physical movement or gesture

And below you will find some of the more specific triggers that individual clients have found useful when choosing their mood.

Trigger	Worth a try?	Before?	During?	Impact on my mood?
I put on lipstick. It says to me, 'Right, in you go – you're ready.'				
I have a selection of playlists I use to trigger different moods. I have a 'get into action playlist', a 'think straight playlist' . . .				

I touch my ring and I
can connect to a feeling
that reminds me that
'I'm enough.'

I wear my father's watch
and it reminds me of his
strength in fighting his
illness – that instantly
powers me up.

I have a toy black cab on
my desk that represents
me at my best in a tricky
conversation I managed
really well in the back of
a cab.

I have a picture that I
carry around of the
whole family together. It
fires me up to make it
happen again.

I draw confidence from
my old Green Beret. I
keep it in my bag to
reconnect with all it
represents in terms of
respect, hard work and
the commando spirit.

I have a picture of my
nephew. I will persevere
through anything for
him.

I have a small Buddha
that a dear friend gave
to me. I hear his
encouragement and it
pushes me forward.

I have a ring that
represents all three of
us: me and my children.
We will do it together.

Travelling to work,
listening to tunes that
make my head bounce,
is so necessary to set me
up for success. These
are all songs that make
me feel 10 feet tall. They
all have a certain beat
and tempo that I feel
dictates me at my best.

What's yours?

SELF-TALK

If you're on stage and it's not going well, the
audience will tell you – by God they will.
Sometimes it feels like they've got together in
the foyer to decide not to laugh. But then it's
wonderful, because it's like you're in the middle
of a range of mountains and you think, 'I'm not
going to be beaten by this. I'm going to try and
do it better.'

Dame Judi Dench

We *all* engage in self-talk. For those of you who think you
don't have an inner voice, it's the one telling you that.

So how can being more deliberate about our self-talk
help us choose our mood?

Alan told me he wanted to be better at managing his
Dog brain. 'I can't seem to control the way I feel when
things get tough in meetings. I give myself a hard time
and then I can't think straight.'

I asked him to describe what had happened in his most
recent tricky meeting.

We were stuck in treacle . . . I was meant to be chairing
the meeting and it was becoming almost impossible to
manage. We needed to reach a decision as a collective and
it was getting increasingly tense.
My self-talk went into overdrive and got louder: *You've
got to get a grip here. People are rambling, going over anecdotal
evidence which everyone's building on. We're losing so much time –
I should move us on but we're right in the teeth of it.*

He went on to say: 'I could feel all my energy being drained from trying to control my conversation with me rather than with the people in the room. I was exhausting myself.'

Alan was spot on. What we say to ourselves can be very exhausting. As another client said to me recently, 'I get on my own nerves. It's relentless.' In pressured situations, self-talk can either propel us into anxiety, exhausting us, or propel us into action, enabling us to exert greater self-discipline. The choice is ours. Under pressure, though, making that choice is hard.

Alan believed he would be a better chair if he could be more positive with his self-talk. He just didn't know how.

I asked him to connect to a recent trophy moment – perhaps one where he had faced a similar challenge. I then asked him to recall the specific skills he had brought to that moment. As often happens when clients connect to a moment of appreciation and pride, the body responds first. It can't help it. It's often very subtle and I love to look out for it. In Alan's case he literally broadened, his face softened and his words took on a relaxed tone. 'The moment I'm thinking about isn't work-related and I feel strange even calling it a trophy moment – but it was. I managed to pull together a fractious family situation after the death of my mother. In order to fulfil her wishes, I had to remain calm and curious but strong with all the family members.'

We agreed it might be worth connecting to that trophy moment and create a self-talk to help him choose his mood when necessary. Every time he needed to boost his confidence he would simply say to himself, 'Stay calm, curious and strong.'

He found that connecting to this new self-talk allowed him to focus on what was happening in the meeting – rather than in his head – and he had more control in those tricky moments.

Sometimes, something as simple as a shift in language, altering how we choose to talk to ourselves, can help us feel better and move forward faster, with more energy.

Juliet is a good example of this. She had just stepped into the role of finance director and was the only woman on the board. We met because she wanted to be better at sharing her opinion earlier in board meetings. She said, 'I sit there, and even though I have all the data in front of me, I say to myself, *You really aren't as good as these guys*, and I remain quiet for far too long.'

As Juliet described her self-talk, I noticed that her inner voice was addressing her as *You*.

I asked, 'Who's that speaking?'

She looked at me, slightly bemused.

I continued, 'I'm wondering if it's actually you talking?'

Without thinking she blurted, with a laugh, 'No. You know what? It's my old Maths teacher. Can you believe it?'

I suggested that, next time her inner voice pitched in,

she could try replacing the *You* with *Juliet* to see if that made a difference.

At our second meeting, she couldn't wait to tell me how it had gone. 'I was in this tricky meeting and, sure enough, that voice started again: *You can't do this.* So I paused and tried what we had agreed. As I said to myself, *Juliet can't do this*, I just got angry and thought, *Hang on a minute, that's not right actually. Yes, Juliet bloody can.* At which point, I felt a surge of energy, leaned in and piped up.'

Replacing the pronoun with her first name helped Juliet. It may be helpful for you too – if you want to offload a rogue teacher.

There's been some interesting research into the language used in our self-talk, particularly on how it can enhance our self-control. At the Emotion & Self Control Laboratory, run by psychologist Ethan Kross at the University of Michigan, eighty-nine participants were asked to give a speech about why they were perfectly qualified for their ideal job. Everyone had five minutes to prepare. One group was told to use only pronouns in their prep documents, while the other was told to use their names. The ones using only pronouns became a lot more anxious as they prepared, saying things like 'How can I possibly write a speech in five minutes?' The others displayed less anxiety as they prepared, encouraging themselves instead. Further confirmation came when they presented their speeches. Those using their name were judged to have performed better and afterwards were able to move on more quickly, chewing over the bad bits less. Kross explains, 'When dealing with strong emotions, taking a step back and becoming a detached observer can help.' He goes on, 'It's very easy for people to advise their friends, yet, when it comes to themselves, they have trouble. People engaging in this process, using their own first name, are distancing themselves from the self, right in the moment, and that helps them perform.'

It's funny how other people can unhelpfully take up lodgings in our head and remain there far too long – without us even realizing. Many people I work with have a 'guest' that has long outstayed their welcome. Some even have more than one.

Maggie was a lawyer who described the pressure she placed on herself as 'two small girls who sit on each of my shoulders and whisper'. She seemed to know them very well. She described how they dressed, sat, stood, even what they did with their hands. 'They have fun on my shoulders. It's like they know something I don't and they take pride in that. They whisper about all the possible things that can go wrong. They tell me how I might mess up, or they just sit smugly with their hands folded and reprimand me for having the arrogance to even believe I could do it in the first place.'

We could have spent a lot of time understanding these 'girls' – how they got there and all the possible reasons why. We didn't. What was important was that Maggie acknowledged them. She'd personalized them.

I asked if the girls were ever helpful. She deliberated for a moment and replied, 'Actually, yes. They can alert me to risk, but that's only helpful long *before* the moment of pressure, not *in* it. I need to invite them when I want them.' That was all she needed. To know that they could be useful and that it was her choice.

Having made that decision, she had to find a practical way to execute her choice. Our inner voice rarely waits to be asked its opinion. It helps if we have a practice that enables us to listen when our self-talk is useful and replace it when it's not. A practice that works for us. I say that because Maggie's practice might appear a little odd but, after experimenting with a few possibilities, she eventually landed on one that became instrumental in helping her to be even better under pressure.

Maggie's daily practice

1. She gave the girls names.

2. She would sit them on an imaginary sofa – some distance from her.

3. She took charge. She decided when she listened to them, rather than them speaking without an invitation.

She created another practice for when she had a pressured situation – going into court, for example, or a tough client meeting.

Maggie's pressure practice

1. She would casually brush the top of each shoulder to check they were 'free'. She called it her 'trigger for choice', allowing her to walk in without her pair of 'judges'. She began to have a lot of fun with it.

2. As she walked through the door, she sometimes held it open for a couple of extra seconds to let the two little girls run free and sit outside and wait for her. She'd say to herself, *Go on, you two. Off you go. I don't need you for this.*

3. Then she'd close the door and stride in with a grounded sense of her own confidence.

As I say, to most of us, that seems a bizarre routine. But part of the magic of this kind of practice is that it doesn't have to make sense to anyone else – or even to you for that matter. It just has to work and be repeatable – providing incremental small adjustments that help you to move closer to your goal.

Some of the self-talk traps that we can get caught in may seem insurmountable at first. As we focus on the reasons why something or someone is impossible, we become experts at running critical commentaries – about ourselves, those around us or the world – using phrases like *I'm never heard, There's no point trying, I'm hopeless at this, She always does that, They're trying to catch me out*. These commentaries are often well-rehearsed and familiar to us. As a consequence, they require less energy from us.

Forward-focused self-talk has to be practised. It requires energy to set out on a different course. Sometimes it's easier (and cathartic too) to moan to others, blame ourselves, blame others and contexts rather than choose to take action and do something different.

The characteristics of useful self-talk that I suggest you focus on, therefore, need to be realistically optimistic. Focus on what is in your control. Be solution-focused. Say it enough for it to feel more familiar and then, to quote the remarkable American educator Rita Pierson, 'You say it long enough, it starts to be part of you and live in you.'

When Rita was handed a class with very poor academic ability, one of the first things she did was give them a mantra – a statement to repeat, both as a class and on their own:

> I am somebody. I was somebody when I came. I'll be a better somebody when I leave. I am powerful, and I am strong. I deserve the education that I get here. I have things to do, people to impress, and places to go.

A well-publicized example from the world of tennis is Andy Murray's self-talk in the 2012 US Open after he'd let a two-set lead slip and, after four sets, appeared destined to continue the pattern and lose his fifth consecutive grand-slam final. He took a toilet break to regain his focus. That toilet break has now become a famous 'shift moment'.

I stood in front of the mirror with sweat dripping down my face and I knew I had to change what was going on inside . . . So I started talking. Out loud. 'You are not losing this match,' I said to myself. 'You are not losing this match.' I started out a little tentative but my voice got louder. 'You are not going to let this one slip . . . This is your time.' . . . At first it felt a bit weird, but I felt something change inside. I was surprised by my response. I knew I could win.

He did. And a month later he won at the Olympics too.

Now, I'm sure Mr Kross would have liked him to have started that self-talk not with 'You' but with 'Andy'. Furthermore, if I were being really picky, I would have preferred him to replace 'You are not losing' with 'You are winning this match.' I have witnessed how focusing on what you want rather than what you don't want can make a tangible difference to people's ability to make progress. Anyone who has tried to guide a toddler will know that saying 'Don't fall off the wall!' is more than likely to cause them to fall. They focus so hard on the *Don't* that they *Do*. The power of the negative. But, hey, it got Murray the result he wanted. He played better through shifting his self-talk towards the outcome he wanted.

Thinking *Don't* tends to undermine our intention.

Some sports coaches actively discourage thinking *Don't*. They suggest that it unhelpfully directs the mind to what's not to be done, and increases the likelihood that the athlete will feel stress and anxiety. This then makes it harder for them to pay attention to the task or skill at hand, making them more prone to do exactly what they hoped to avoid.

Jennie, a teenage lacrosse player, shifted her self-talk for that very reason. 'Positive self-talk has become really important to me in my game,' she said. 'As a forward I'm often under pressure to take a pass and try to score, despite the attention of aggressive defenders and their sticks. My old self-talk was "Don't drop it" as I saw another pass hurtling towards me. On reflection, this was getting in my way. Now my self-talk is "Catch it. Score." This has helped me feel much more confident in tight games and, I'm glad to say, I'm definitely scoring more goals!'

When we focus specifically on what we want, it invites all three of our brains to act and think forward – about what is possible instead of what isn't. My daughter headed off to start her AS year feeling positively challenged and excited at the prospect of her learning journey. After an introductory Spanish A-level lesson that began with a list of *Don'ts*, she returned home saying, 'I sat there feeling butterflies in my stomach, thinking, *I've made the wrong choice and I'm never going to pass this.*'

Malala Yousafzai, the world-renowned activist for women's education, recounts the self-talk she used as a teenager when preparing for the possibility of encountering the Taliban. She could have said to herself, 'Don't acknowledge them, don't let them scare you, don't give in.' She didn't.

'I asked myself, "If the Taliban comes, what would you do, Malala?" Then I would reply to myself, "Malala, just take a shoe and hit him."' There speaks the youngest ever Nobel Prize winner. It's interesting to note that not only did her self-talk focus on Do thoughts rather than Don'ts, but she also used her own name, something that, according to Kross, would have provided some distance to help regulate her strong emotions.

So, I invite you to get curious about your own self-talk. What do you say to yourself under pressure? Does it help you to be better? Sometimes when I'm in the gym and I'm really struggling to complete that last twenty-second sprint on the sadistic Curve machine, I tell myself that my children's lives depend on me finishing it. Lucky for them I do. It helps me to persevere. The language we use has the power to affect our performance and our effort.

Professor Samuel Marcora, Director of Research at the School of Sport and Exercise Sciences at the University of Kent, began an enquiry into fatigue, addressing questions like 'What is it?' and 'What sets its limits?' He conducted a series of experiments with athletes on bicycles. His research revealed that the athletes' performance improved by 17 per cent when they heard subliminal words like *go* and *lively* as opposed to words like *toil* and *sleep*. When the athletes heard these motivating words, their perception of effort was reduced and their capacity increased without them even being aware of it.

Paying more attention to our self-talk can widen our perspective about how much better we can be – in whatever way works for us. So, experiment. Become aware of what you say and have a play with other soundtracks. What works well might surprise you. Take Karen, for example.

Fed up with constantly chastising herself for not achieving enough in a day, Karen tried a completely different approach. 'I began the day saying to myself, *Karen, do as little as possible*. To my astonishment I had a very productive day.'

To summarize, self-talk is a useful ingredient in every aspect of deliberately getting better. Choosing our self-talk can boost our confidence, calm our Dog brain and free us up to perform at our best. Becoming more aware of how we talk to ourselves is often the first step.

It's worth choosing the most useful self-talk in advance – anticipating before we experience the pressure. That way we can conserve the mind energy our Human brain needs in order to focus on what's going on outside of our own head.

Here are the three steps that clients find most useful in choosing better self-talk:

Step 1	Become curious and listen to what you say to yourself.
Step 2	Press Pause on unhelpful self-talk.
Step 3	Replace it with something more forward-focused. Choose a positive, energizing mantra to stay strong, and connect it to something that really matters to you. (If you have thought about this in advance, it is much easier to call upon it in a moment of pressure.)

Below are some examples of how others have used self-talk to choose their mood. Try them and see if any help you.

Self-talk	Worth a try?	Before?	During?	Impact on my mood?
When I feel like I'm going to snap at my kids, I say to myself, Step into parent. I'm the parent.				
Whenever I say, 'I can't,' I press Pause and replace it with I'll have a go.				

When he irritates me
I say to myself, Stay
calm. Keep listening.

If that lack of
confidence creeps in
I remind myself, I have
managed great teams
before.

When I think of
setting up my own
business, I put my
hands together and
say, I can do it and
I will.

When running gets
hard I say, Long
strides – light and
easy.

Every time I think
I have to do better or
try harder, I stop and
gently say, Relaxed
confidence.

When I realize I'm
talking too fast and
for too long, I say to
myself, Take a Pinot
Noir moment.

When I feel furious,
I tell myself, Remain
light and breezy.

After several bruising
meetings drove me to
lie low, I imagined
myself making a
confident re-entry,
saying to myself,
I'm back!

When I waste my
energy dwelling on
personal hurts, I say
to myself, It's part of
my role as CEO to be
exposed to this.

When I feel tempted
to gossip, I say to
myself Blurt outside
the business, be
curious inside.

When I get tongue-
tied, I think, Remain
in pitch mode.

When I put myself
under pressure, I say,
Stay listening and
relax.

When I'm over-tired,
frustrated and late to
leave, I tell myself,
My health matters.
Be properly selfish.

Nervous about the
day ahead, I just
remind myself, I
deserve to be where
I am. I then feel ready
to face the day of
work.

What's yours?

SUMMARY

When we want to choose our mood, rather than have our
Reptile and Dog brains choose it for us, it takes deliberate
effort. It takes effort to first pause and then override their
fast urges and impulses. Body posture, breath, appreciation, triggers and self-talk are practical tools we can use
to interrupt the force and speed of our Reptile and Dog
brains. Whether you practise just one or all five, they will
require regular and deliberate practise until they become
habitual. This is particularly important when, as we will
see in the next chapter, we are under pressure.

Better Under Pressure

6.

CHOOSE CONTROL

Before we move on to the next energy, let's take a closer look at pressure. Pressure can be a useful force. It pushes us to stretch beyond what we thought we were capable of. But while making a considered choice requires some effort, making that choice under pressure requires even more. To do so successfully, you have to anticipate, prepare and rehearse for it.

Making better choices under pressure means giving the Human brain the chance to focus, whatever unexpected distraction or shock comes our way. This focus requires extra effort (and ideally a well-stocked SHED). When we have a practice that automatically kicks in each time we encounter pressure, we can engage the Human brain rather than being at the mercy of our instinctive and impulsive animal brains which will choose for us and leave us feeling out of control and bewildered.

Studies into people who survive this type of pressure situation offer interesting insights on the importance of mood and making a deliberate plan. The research shows that people who have survived extraordinary circumstances the best spend very little time focusing on what has been lost or gone wrong. They deliberately focus instead on a plan to survive. This enables the Human brain to manage the potentially disastrous urges and impulses of the animal brains.

Recent research on this subject can be found in Amanda Ripley's *The Unthinkable*, a study of ordinary people who have survived some of the world's most harrowing catastrophes. Ripley's book shows just how important it is to control 'inbuilt and instinctive reactions' so as to apply 'cautious deliberation and to make good decisions'.

For me, feeling in control is the key to handling pressure.

As a family we experienced something akin to this when we visited a beach outside Cape Town in South Africa. Our nine-year-old son, Charlie, had been standing up to his ankles at the edge of a relatively lively sea, watching the waves crash against some nearby rocks. Before we knew it, he'd been caught in a rip current and, within what seemed like seconds, had been pulled out of his depth and was struggling to keep his head above the water. My husband instinctively ran into the sea after him and, before he knew it, was in trouble himself, unable to stay above water. Thankfully – and I remain grateful to him to this day – a surfer (I don't even know his name) had seen the drama unfold, waded across, scooped Charlie on to his board and yelled to Chris to swim with the waves parallel to the beach towards the rocks. Both were saved.

For my part, throughout the ordeal, I found myself guarding our daughter on the beach, frantically pacing in smaller and smaller circles, totally confused about what to do and feeling absolutely helpless.

I have relived the whole experience many times. Just thinking about it makes my heart quicken. As I replay it, I see Chris become primeval in his focus on saving his child. Chris's strong paternal instinct impelled him to take a foolhardy, dangerous decision and rush into the sea, where he nearly drowned too. The surfer's advice was totally counter-intuitive, but luckily Chris followed it.

Under pressure, the sequence is always the same. We respond physically first as our instinctive and intuitive habits take over – urging and impelling us to act without running it by our Human brain first. Under pressure, our fast-acting, well-intentioned instincts and intuitions may not always be as useful as our slower, more deliberate, Human-brain decisions.

It was my first year as a teacher. I was halfway through my immaculately planned lesson on Elizabethan theatre, eagerly trying to engage a class of fifteen-year-olds, when a voice from the back of the class boomed, 'Miss, this lesson is f**king boring.'

My heart began pounding. The entire class had gone silent. They all waited to see if I would pass this test. *What's she going to do? Go on, miss, prove yourself.*

Meanwhile, Wayne – the instigator of my internal chaos with his honest appraisal – was slumped in his chair, arms folded defiantly, awaiting my response. I realized that I hadn't been trained for this scenario. My teacher training simply hadn't taught me how to deal with someone who wanted to derail my lessons like this.

My head battled with indecision. What next? Did I:

- Throw him out, fill in a report, send him to the head, etc.?

- Run for the hills?

- Do something else?

The pressure felt immense. My credibility within the class – which I'd been working so hard to cultivate over the last few months – could be blown sky high. I had to do something – quickly. Looking back, I see that this was the point where any impulsive, emotional response was interrupted. Standing still, I paused and looked straight at Wayne. I found myself calmly saying: 'Wayne – it really isn't my desire to come to work and be f**king boring. Please tell me how I can make it more interesting for you.'

I'd love to say that in that moment I had thought my actions through – but I can't. I hadn't. For a start, I'd sworn back at him. Definitely not one of the recommended behaviour management strategies in my postgraduate course, and clear grounds for dismissal if I were to do it today.

Wayne looked stunned. The tension in that moment felt unbearable. The class turned their gaze to Wayne, then back at me. I remember thinking, *Stay still. Breathe. Keep calm and be interested in his response.*

Wayne looked up. 'I dunno. That's your job, isn't it?'

Giggles around the class. I persisted with the question and offered it out to everyone else.

'I'm serious. Do tell me how I can make it more interesting. I want to know. What does anyone else think? Any ideas?'

I could sense my heart rate dropping as people answered. Not Wayne, admittedly, but others were entering the dialogue.

'Why are we doing Elizabethan drama? It's boring.'

'Can't you make it more practical?'

Wayne's silence was screaming at me. Eventually he looked up. 'How is knowing about the Elizabethans going to help me get a job?'

This unleashed more honest views in the room. They

were difficult to hear. Up went my heart rate again. I could feel myself taking it all very personally, but I forced myself to listen.

The lesson eventually ended, and Wayne and his mates headed out. I was relieved and emotionally exhausted. I'd survived. Not sure exactly how, but I had.

Fast forward: the following lessons with the class were better. There was more openness and camaraderie, as if we had got through something together. Wayne contributed more positively and I changed the way I planned my lessons.

With the benefit of hindsight, there were two key ingredients that helped me manage myself in my interaction with Wayne: my breath and my posture. I hadn't consciously chosen either.

My past experience of performing under pressure had helped me – particularly as a child, enduring violin exams, which were always hideously nerve-racking. I had been taught week in, week out, to anticipate the exam conditions and their likely impact on my ability to perform. To manage my nerves, my teacher made me practise standing tall and breathing out slowly. That would keep my hand from shaking as I held the bow so the examiner would see me play at my best. I had been trained to manage myself under exam pressure. I had been so drilled in it that in my hour of need, in front of that class, it was my automatic response that came to my rescue.

My lesson with Wayne happened a long time ago. Since

then I have met other 'Waynes'. I work with people who are put under pressure by Waynes of their own. Colleagues, bosses, children, friends, parents. We all have a Wayne somewhere. We hope they'll be quiet, shut up or go away. They rarely do.

When they don't and you haven't anticipated and prepared yourself, it's high risk. As Carol, a senior executive in a global company discovered . . .

She had a monthly board meeting with, among others, one significant stakeholder.

'I will never forget it – not only because of the way he behaved, but more importantly how I behaved.'

According to Carol, no sooner had the meeting begun than he set about eviscerating her in front of the senior management, the international senior management and significant members of the finance team. She told me his attitude was dismissive, aggressive and belittling. To her, it sounded like: *You don't know what you're doing. You don't understand our business. I would've been doing XYZ by now. Why haven't you?* Carol felt it was patently obvious to everyone at the meeting that he didn't want her in that job. He wanted her off that team and someone else on his team promoted into her role. That someone else was in the room and this man was taking this public opportunity to prove his point.

According to Carol, the tirade got worse and worse and she, in turn, became smaller and smaller, quieter and quieter. She became less clear, less coherent, more disorganized in her thinking, increasingly unable to stand her ground, to defend her position or articulate an alternative view.

Carol told me there had been fourteen people in the room besides the two of them and not one person uttered a word. Some 'switched off', some even started dealing with emails. No one said anything. Unsurprisingly, afterwards people dropped her commiserating emails, but the damage had already been done. To make matters worse, another meeting was due the following month.

'I knew I had to change. I had to find a way to manage myself with this person,' Carol told me.

She asked me to help set her up for that next meeting. The man was clearly unpredictable, so we had to prepare for his unpredictability. We built some techniques to keep her Human brain in play – whatever he did next time. We planned for many different possibilities. What if he:

- Said nothing?
- Shouted and swore?

- Shut her down?

- Belittled someone else?

- Even . . . arrived and apologized?

Key professions spend a great deal of time training for the pressure of the unexpected – especially when a mistake could prove fatal. The military originated a term for such training: *dislocated expectations*. This has since been adopted by all sorts of organizations – from the business world right through to the England rugby team. The key principle is that they become more adaptable as they understand and actively expect that something unexpected will happen to change the plan – however robust.

Carol and I agreed to spend time anticipating as many scenarios as possible so we could minimize any potential shock, lessen anxiety, decide how she would respond in each situation and rehearse it. Even if something took place that wasn't exactly one of these scenarios, Carol would be better prepared to deal with the unexpected and be more confident to adapt. By doing this, we reduced the sense of novelty that the Dog and Reptile brains are so alert to. They would therefore be more inclined to let the Human brain back into play, allowing Carol to remain calm and focused under pressure.

Having first anticipated as many scenarios as she could, I then encouraged her to reflect on how she wished to be in each one, asking her:

- What is your most useful body posture to remain calm and in control?

- What else would help you feel confident in that moment?

- In that confident state – what do you want to say?

By this point, Carol felt she was prepared. This is a common misunderstanding: the idea that thinking it through is enough. Under pressure it isn't – and she wasn't.

Having defined her responses, we tested them – in the safety of her office, of course. I adopted his attitude for each different scenario, mirroring his unpredictability as best I could, making it as real as possible so she could put her planned reaction into practice. This is a crucial step: saying it out loud, practising it as if it is actually happening. Through doing that, we had reassured Carol's Reptile and Dog brains that, even if an unexpected scenario were to happen, Carol would be better prepared to deal with it.

The next meeting finally arrived.

On one side of the table sat Carol and her three colleagues. Over half an hour late, *he* walked in bringing, unexpectedly, seven people with him. At this point, Carol's Finance Director stood up and went to join him, sitting opposite her. (A scenario we had not predicted!) Carol prepared herself to present the purpose of the meeting, the goals and what they hoped to achieve. She could already feel the tension and silence in the room.

Indeed – as per a scenario we did predict – no sooner had she begun than she was interrupted.

'BULLSHIT! This is the worst fucking budget I've ever seen. It's a fairy tale. You've been in this job for a year now and you've no idea what you're doing. You and your team are a joke . . .'

A seven-minute tirade followed about how hopeless the team was.

'I don't know why I had thought he would be any different this time,' Carol told me later. 'But I was.'

Having anticipated this outburst and prepared for it, Carol was able to let him speak while she sat there calmly, feet placed firmly on the floor, saying nothing. At one point, one of her colleagues went to say something but Carol gently signalled them not to.

When the tirade had finished, Carol focused on a subtle, slow exhalation and then calmly said, 'Are we going to have a budget meeting or not?'

Carol told me, 'He looked at me and, for the first time, I saw a flicker of "I might have got this wrong." I remained composed and waited quietly. Then, still looking at me, he said "Or not!" Then he stood and walked out, closely followed by his team.'

Carol had anticipated and developed what we called her 'Under Pressure Practice' to cope with her Wayne. Waynes require you to do that in order to handle them. We all know logically that when someone says something unpleasant about us, the impulsive instinct to strike a blow or to freeze is less useful now than 2,000 years ago. But engaging the human brain in this moment of choice is not easy. That's where the effort comes in. Having a practical method to override the fast, automatic urges and impulses that want to take over can return us to a neutral position and allow us to pause and choose more deliberately what we actually want to do.

SO, WHAT'S YOUR UNDER PRESSURE PRACTICE?

Many clients have found it invaluable to deliberately prepare an 'Under Pressure Practice'. Here are a few examples.

Abi, a member of our team, also works as a sports pre-senter on TV. A lot of her work involves interviewing and getting the best from boxers, cyclists, rugby players and motor-racers. They often do not wish to be interviewed straight after the match or race – especially if they've lost. She needs to be ready for their unpredictability. This is her routine before going on air – to help her remain 'strong and agile'.

Body posture	I start with my feet. Place them firmly on the ground. Own my space. I imagine a smile across my chest.
Breath	Two deep breaths – three beats in through the nose and seven beats out.

Appreciation	I connect to my first live interview in the pit lane at the French Grand Prix when everything just clicked and I performed at my absolute best. I recall a strong visual image of myself with the driver.
Trigger	I have a small Buddha in my pocket that I always touch before I start. I had it for that first interview and I carry it always.
Self-talk	'Bring the viewers' heroes to life in their living room.'

We met Steve Williams, another member of our team, earlier. A double Olympic champion in the British rowing fours from both Athens (2004) and Beijing (2008), he describes the moment when he and the rest of his team were waiting on the start line at the Olympic final as 'the longest six minutes of our lives'.

He and his team's routine to stay in control was as follows:

Body posture	Sit like the champion. Sit up tall in the boat.
Breath	Take slow, deep breaths to oxygenate the blood and send signals to the brain that we are not under threat here, we are in control.
Appreciation	Focus on our personal best – our fastest time: 2:47 for 1,000 metres.

Trigger	We all kept tapping one another on the shoulder or squeezing the foot of the guy behind us to remind ourselves we're in this together.
Self-talk:	'We were the ones who did 2:47 last week and we can do it again!'

They won gold in both Olympics. In the 2004 games by the narrowest margin, just 0.08 of a second – or, as the *Daily Mail* put it, 'the length of a Crunchie bar'!

Whether or not you are trying to be an Olympic champion, using an Under Pressure Practice can make an incremental difference to your performance and help you be better. It's whatever works for you to help manage you under pressure.

Here are some examples of how others have employed their practice. Some use all five elements in sequence, others use only a few. See if any work for you.

Example 1 *Every time I head towards an interview I really want, I can literally feel the pressure mounting in my body and I start to worry about everything that can go wrong. So, I focus on my body and what I say to myself:*

Body posture	Walk tall – open shoulders.
Breath	Two calm and steady exhalations – breathing out the nerves.

Trigger	I touch the chain my mum gave me to connect to her belief in me.
Self-talk:	'I've done the work – I'm ready.'

Example 2 *Any judgement on me is a huge derailment. I go into victim mode and become quiet or shut down. I shift myself into useful action mode like this:*

Body posture	Change position. It doesn't matter how, just change it.
Breath	Breathe out slowly.
Self-talk	'Right! Out of victim and into a positive plan.'

Example 3 *I have meetings with this maddening colleague. I know this is a strong reaction but I'd really prefer her not to be in my life. She makes my blood boil. The time I waste with her is better off spent elsewhere. When she speaks or fails to respond to an email, I focus on doing this:*

Body posture	Shoulders back.
Breath	Breathe out slowly for the count of seven – slow and gently.
Trigger	The water – sailing on the sea, which I love. Feeling free and connecting to being in control of the boat – cutting through the water.
Self-talk	'Do nothing immediately!'

Example 4 *My Under Pressure Practice has been invaluable as a junior doctor in my final year. I am continually overseen while I examine patients, which is nerve-racking, and I feel the pressure. So:*

Body posture	I walk calmly into the cubicle and greet the patient and the examiner with a smile.
Breath	Two deep breaths – three beats in through the nose and seven beats out.
Appreciation	I reconnect to the exhilaration and confidence I feel when I am skiing.
Trigger	I touch the crinkly paper in my pocket to connect me to the snow.
Self-talk	'I'm a great skier, I'm going to be a great doctor.'

Once clients have found their Under Pressure Practices, I work with them and slowly increase the pressure as they rehearse their practice. In the world of theatre, there is a well-trodden route to the ultimate pressure of the press night. The actors begin rehearsals with the script in their hands, they repeat scenes over and over, pausing regularly for the director to give them notes and refine the piece. Then they rehearse without the script. At a particular point, they rehearse with the props and their costume. Then they move into the actual theatre space and have a technical rehearsal, followed by a dress rehearsal and even a handful of preview performances – all building towards the opening night and the pressure of the critics' reviews. Each stage in the process increases the pressure little by little until they feel ready to deliver a confident performance, tell the story most effectively and move their audience.

Anticipating, preparing and rehearsing strengthens your ability to deal with pressure and helps with any unexpected 'curve balls'. It is what all emergency services do to train their front-line people. Exposure to pressure is a critical part of the learning process. The more familiar the three brains are with the situation, the more they allow you to execute your intended plan.

Follow this three-step approach for your own Under Pressure Practice:

ANTICIPATE	What might happen? Consider all possible 'what if' scenarios.
PREPARE	For each scenario, consider: What you will do. What you will say.
REHEARSE	Act out each scenario: Say it out loud!

Our Five Energies

Body Energy

Mood Energy

Mind Energy

Purpose Energy

People Energy

7.

CHOOSE TO FOCUS

'Anyone can get angry – that is easy. But to do this with the right person, to the right extent, at the right time, with the right motive, and in the right way, that is not for everyone, nor is it easy.'

Aristotle

As we have seen in the last two chapters, directing our emotions in the most useful way takes deliberate effort. It's hard.

Mind energy is what we use to make deliberate decisions. To make choices.

Concentrating on reading this book and choosing to apply any of the practices will require your mind energy. If, by now, you've chosen a new SHED practice or one to become better at choosing your mood, it will take your mind energy to practise it enough to develop it into a habit. Choosing to learn any new skill requires our focused attention, sustained effort and time.

Our Dog and Reptile brains are driven simply to direct our attention to whatever gives us the most immediate satisfaction. They make it harder for the Human brain to slow us down, exercise self-control, and apply focused concentration and effort – mind energy.

As I'm writing, the sun is out, I can smell the coffee that my husband is brewing downstairs and I'd love to just abandon the writing and go and join him. In fact, I could

quickly nip to the shop and buy a couple of cheeky crois-
sants and a newspaper and sit with him in the garden. I
can feel the pull of my Dog and Reptile brains. They are
urging me, *Go on, get downstairs. You know it will be more fun.*

Becoming more deliberate is so much more challenging
since all sorts of tempting options surround us. Our Dog
and Reptile brains seduce us into thinking that an extra
thirty minutes in bed, rather than eating any breakfast, will
help us be more effective in the day. Or sorting our emails
into folders, so avoiding a pressing, complex proposal that
needs addressing, will help clear our heads. Succumbing to
the pull of our animal brains – getting distracted by something easier – gives us a sense of instant gratification.
Choosing a different course often requires self-control,
willpower and concentration – mind energy.

In this instance, I manage to resist their pull by making
a deal with them. *If I give myself thirty more minutes of focused
work, then I'll reward myself with a coffee break in the sun.*

Mind energy is the energy that our Human brain uses
to concentrate, imagine, solve problems, be creative, build
relationships – and listen, *really* listen, with genuine curiosity. All of which set us humans apart. Making considered
decisions to focus on an intent or activity – setting up a
new TV, learning a new language or sport, making time
to buy those tickets, having a meaningful conversation,
doing your tax return, planning a trip, saving money or
writing a proposal – uses mind energy.

Using our mind energy is tiring. So, it's important to
make good choices about where and how to direct it. Even

when we know what we want to achieve, it's essential to prioritize where we place our effort and focus on useful practices, in a useful sequence.

Ironically, the effort of making one decision actively affects our energy to make the next one, and so on. *Decision fatigue* is now a recognized term.

Thankfully, most of us don't have to decide how to walk or get ourselves dressed. Deciding *what* to wear, however – that is a whole other thing and uses up mind energy (and can make me late). To conserve my energy for the day ahead, I have to think about it deliberately the night before. Former president Barack Obama – with all the responsibility and decision-making his job entailed – took conserving his mind energy one step further. As he told *Vanity Fair*:

> I wear only gray or blue suits. I'm trying to pare down decisions. I don't want to make decisions about what I'm eating or wearing because I have too many other decisions to make . . . You need to focus your decision-making energy. You need to routinize yourself. You can't be going through the day distracted by trivia.

Getting better at anything requires sustained mind effort and concentration – especially in the early stages. Remember your first few driving lessons? Luckily you have an expert in the car with you, guiding you, helping you focus on useful practices, in a useful sequence. Effectively prioritizing for you. Your Human brain is working to focus on each of these new practices. At the same time, it's trying to manage the urges and impulses from the other two brains. Neither of them will know anything about the skill of driving a car, but they may well get excited by the sense of freedom or worry about hitting the kerb or become flustered when you stall at the lights. *Eeeeeek, here comes another roundabout!*

Most of us are trying to manage urges and impulses like these on a daily basis – and often failing miserably. In the process of writing this book, I know what I should be doing and I have spent hours *not* doing it.

As my client Calvin said at the start of one meeting, 'If I could stop getting so easily distracted I know I could achieve so much more. I just can't seem to stay focused on the main thing. There are too many main things.'

On some level, most of the people I work alongside know what they want to do, yet there is often a gap between knowing it and doing it.

We've all experienced the Know/Do Gap at some point. We know we want to do something and even know

what to do, but still end up not having done it maybe a day, a week or even a month later. Or we know what we want to do but don't know how to start. It's just easier not to.

Mind energy helps us close this gap, and although it takes a lot of effort – for all of us – the good news is we can get better at the way we apply it.

To apply our mind energy, it helps if we can create the conditions that we find most conducive. I am constantly intrigued by the ways in which successful people create their ideal conditions – however odd – to summon and sustain mind energy. To focus and get stuff done.

In his fascinating book on rituals, Mason Currey examines how some of the world's most famous creative minds organized their lives to increase their ability to accomplish what they wanted – people such as Sylvia Plath, Benjamin Franklin, Igor Stravinsky, Mark Twain and Friedrich Schiller. Their methods ranged from rising early at the same time every day (Plath) to spending the morning naked (Franklin); from standing on one's head (Stravinsky) to reading the day's work to one's family over dinner (Twain). Schiller even found focus from smelling a drawer of decaying apples. The main lesson of the book is that there's no one way to get things done. In all these examples, the act – through repetition – became a routine. As Currey says, 'A solid routine fosters a well-worn groove for one's mental energies.' It's for each of us to discover what works best for us.

So, what's your routine? What works best for you? For me, having a candle burning with a specific smell helps – so that has become an essential part of my routine. Smell is a particularly powerful enabler for me. Although decaying apples is probably a step too far.

When clients want to create better conditions to apply their mind energy, I often ask them to think of a time when they found something effortless. It might've been because of their interest in the topic, or because they'd unwittingly chanced upon something that made their ability to focus easier. Often, through that enquiry, they begin to identify a few key ingredients that made it feel effortless.

Becoming more of a scientist around your own behaviour and getting increasingly curious about your own conditions for success will enable you to notice them so that you can then deliberately repeat them.

Here are a few of the top contenders that really help people apply their mind energy:

- Doing exercise beforehand.
- Connecting what needs doing to something that matters to them.
- Deciding on a short deadline.
- Reducing distractions.
- Getting really clear about the end result.
- Making a promise to someone.
- Using the same time (when they're at their best) each day.
- Finding the most conducive space to focus.

And here are some personal practices that my clients have found useful in helping them to focus:

- I get away from the open-plan environment and book a room on another floor with natural light – and I know no one can interrupt me.

- I have a sign I put on my desk saying, *This is a distraction-free zone.*

- I go to a favourite café across the park where I set myself up to complete a particular task in a specific time – with a cup of coffee.

- I give myself a thirty-minute deadline to get through emails efficiently without distraction. When it finishes, I stop.

- I have worked with my PA to put protected focused preparation time in my diary.

- I deliberately say to myself, *Focus on this one small thing and complete it.*

- I take 10 minutes to meditate before I start work.

- I leave my phone in a different room and set my alarm for 90 minutes of focused revision on a clear table.

- I get up at 6 a.m. and do the important (and often harder) things before 10 a.m.

- I focus best when I know everyone else has gone to bed. I can work in a quiet house.

- I connect the value of what I need to do to someone other than me. Their picture close to hand really helps.

- I have no meetings before 10 a.m. All work that demands deep thinking happens before then.

- I promise my family that I will finish by a particular time.

- I have a clear plan for the day with allocated time for each thing I want to get done.

- I arrange to go out with friends or family so have to get it done beforehand.

So, what does it take to apply mind energy to focus deliberately on getting better at something?

A lot of people I work with know that what they are currently doing isn't getting them the results they want and are looking for a new way. They want to apply their mind energy to choose and build a new habit to impact positively on their lives but they don't know how to. In other words, they want to know how to bridge their Know/Do Gap.

The science of getting better is captured in a tome entitled *The Cambridge Handbook of Expertise and Expert Performance*. In this work, leading researchers in the field have identified the key ingredients that create exceptional performance. Interestingly, talent is not one of them. In fact, the ones they *did* identify as essential make for tough reading:

> The journey to truly superior performance is neither for the faint of heart nor for the impatient. The development of genuine expertise requires struggle, sacrifice, and honest, often painful self-assessment. There are no shortcuts.

Bet you can't wait.

Luckily, based on this science, I have come up with a series of simple questions that I regularly ask clients to make becoming better at something feel more fun and feasible. Here they are: seven questions that will help you summon up your mind energy to make better choices; to make 'better' a habit.

1. What is your long-term goal?

Motivated people achieve more. And they do so because they know why their long-term goal matters to them. Strong motivation is essential if you're going to soak up that 'honest, often painful self-assessment' and take on the amount of quality, deliberate practice you'll need.

Knowing and connecting to this long-term goal will help you stay on task. That connection boosts the will to work and consequently the ability to focus. Willpower can be built on a motivation to move towards (*I really want to . . .*) or move away (*I really don't want to . . .*). Both motivate, but moving towards something is often more fun *and* often happens faster. Language is important too. Some like the word *goal*, others prefer *ambition* or even *desire*. It's a personal choice. Fundamentally, the more you can connect to a real goal that matters to you, the more you will be able to harness the power of your will.

Around 2005 I was running a series of sessions with a group of young lawyers who were keen to be better at performing under pressure. Regularly, one senior partner's name cropped up as someone who was difficult to work with and increased the pressure. Most of the participants found him destabilizing and off-putting. However, one young man, Craig, had deliberately chosen a different story:

> I'm working on a case with that partner. The pressure is huge. Yes, he is unreasonable but I knew that before I began working with him. He has a reputation in this firm and that's just how he is. I knew what to expect. He's also very successful and wins a lot. While I don't like the way he treats me, I want to be a successful partner and I'm determined to cope and I'm learning a lot. Yes, I'm exhausted but I know working with him will come to an end, and my CV – and I – will be stronger for the experience.

Craig's ability to tolerate the partner was strengthened because he saw the work as a stepping stone towards his final destination: his long-term goal of becoming a successful partner. Later I asked him why becoming a successful partner mattered to him. He smiled and said, 'I want to be at the top of my profession – it's really important to me.' This ambition motivated him enough to absorb the toughness of the situation, enabling him to build his resilience and remain focused on the task in hand. He viewed it as an opportunity that he could exploit in order to achieve what he wanted in the long term.

There was another participant in the group who was working with the same senior partner. 'He applies unreasonable pressure, in my opinion,' she said. 'He shouts and is personally rude if people have a different view. His behaviour has helped to crystallize what I value in any firm that I would want to be a senior partner in.' I asked her if becoming a senior partner was her long-term goal. She replied, 'Yes, I've always known I wanted to be a senior partner somewhere and I now know it isn't here. This experience has strengthened my resolve to carefully investigate the culture in other firms. I will leave.'

When we have ways to connect to a clear goal that matters, it's easier to put in the effort – effort which clients tend to describe as 'self-control', 'determination', ' drive', 'self-discipline', 'willpower'. Phrases we can all relate to.

Roy Baumeister, a psychologist from Florida University, has studied the concept of self-control/willpower/self-discipline. His research suggests that it is more important than IQ in predicting academic success in young people (I have just told my daughter that).

The clinical psychologist Erica Reischer, in her recent article 'Helping Children Succeed – Without the Stress' for *Atlantic* magazine, supports this idea, suggesting that practising and developing skills related to self-control is proving more effective in schools than tutoring and extra classes. Helping young people inhibit their impulses means they will be better able to remain focused and get the results they want.

Baumeister's research also intimates that self-control and willpower are finite resources that can easily run out. Remember Kate? She lost her temper with her daughter when she spilt the milk. She'd spent all day employing her self-control to avoid reacting negatively to colleagues. By the time she returned home, her self-control was so depleted that her 'Gut to Gob' response took over.

The great news for us (and Kate) is that self-control and willpower, even if finite, can be strengthened. Like any muscle, the more we train them, the stronger they become. We can strengthen them when we connect to our long-term goal and why it really matters to us.

Here are some examples of long-term goals that have helped other people to strengthen their will in order to put in the deliberate effort they needed:

- To set up my own business so I can be autonomous.

- To be in a fulfilling, happy relationship to start a family.

- To be a strong leader for the success of the company.

- To better manage this tricky person so my team are happier and motivated.

- To be a strong presenter so I can motivate others to act.

- To achieve great A levels so I can study where I choose.

- To be fit and healthy to keep my mojo and feel happier.

- To be a professional singer so I can make a living from what I love.

- To be a better dad so my children have a strong role model.

- To sleep more so I can wake up feeling more positive.

You may have the same goal as one (or more) of these people. You may have your own. Either way, if you keep in mind why it matters to you, you can boost your will to continue. Now, question two.

2. What action, skill or routine is the first step towards your goal?

I have met many people who have articulated a strong will to 'be this', or desire to 'do that', but it is by no means a guarantee that it will happen. They might leave me after a meeting, buoyed from having defined what they want, but return next session having done nothing to act on it. My role is to help them select and then define the most useful action or skill for them to focus on (often daily) so that they can make progress towards their long-term goal.

When the GB rowing team — Steve Williams et al. — are in the boat waiting for the Olympic final to start, what do you think they focus on?

1. The gold medal around their neck.

2. The finishing line.

3. A spot ten metres beyond the finishing line.

4. None of the above.

If you chose number 4, well done. It's none of those. In fact, they're trained to focus on the first stroke: the first time their oar hits the water and pulls them into the race. A short-term goal to give them the best possible start towards their long-term goal. Mind energy is most useful when used as a deliberate action energy — focused on the action that will make the most immediate, biggest difference to achieving the long-term goal.

For Steve and his crew-mates, their long-term goal is of course to win the gold medal. It's a wonderful motivation that gets them out of bed for a hard day of training in the middle of winter. Even on Christmas Day. It's not helpful, however, on the start line of the final, when thoughts of the finish will distract their mind energy. Their coach has helped them believe that executing the game plan, starting with a great first stroke, is the key determinant of success. Easy to say; incredibly hard to do. They spend many hours drilling the practice so that, by the time of the final, it's habitual and strong enough to resist any Reptile and Dog distractions.

> Identifying the most useful initial step takes practice. It's a skill in itself.
>
> In the US military, before SEAL recruits start their gruelling training regime, they are actively drilled in the skill of short-term goal-setting. It enables them to change their focus from a fear of the future to just getting through the next few hours. The more pressure they are under, the closer they bring their horizon for the short-term goal. The skill of focusing on getting through the next hour can help them get through the next twenty-four.

Thanks to Steve, I use the term 'first stroke' a lot with clients. They find it very useful when we are working to define their first step. They choose a short-term goal to break their long-term goal down into achievable chunks. It's a skill for Olympians *and* us. Many recreational runners, cyclists and keep-fit people will know the benefits of setting a short-term goal: 'Get out the door'; 'Get to the first lamp post'; 'Just start the workout and see how I go.' And taking on a short-term goal is then easier to turn into sustained effort. The same is even true when tidying up, cutting the grass or washing up after a party. 'Just get the glasses done. Hmm, might as well stack the plates then. Why not clear that? It'll feel good in the morning when I come down to a tidy kitchen.' Once in action, we begin to feel more in control and this helps drive us on.

> As film-maker Ava DuVernay puts it, 'So often I hear people asking, "How do I get started? How do I do this?" You just start. It won't be perfect. It will be messy and it will be hard, but you're doing something and you're on your way.'

And in business, too, a short-term goal can be extremely useful. Leaders who need to tell the rest of their company about a massive and scary change find it a far more manageable prospect when they focus on one conversation at a time.

The skill or action you choose needs careful deliberation. It needs to be realistic, achievable and the most useful one en route to your long-term goal.

My daughter loves singing and has always wanted to be a singer. When she was younger she would sing and sing, desperately hoping to get better without really knowing what she was doing. Then we bought her some lessons with a professional singing coach, Harriette. In the very first lesson, she taught my daughter how to breathe properly and use her breath to support her voice. Immediately, she saw and felt real improvement.

Her long-term goal: to be a singer.

Her first action: learning better breathing techniques.

This first action helped her to progress faster than all the self-initiated practice she had done previously. She was lucky enough to have an expert on hand to guide her and help her prioritize the breathing to get her started. Normally we have to try to prioritize on our own.

Malcolm wanted to write a book. He'd wanted to for several months. He had created an inspiring, stimulating environment at the bottom of his garden to work in. He called it his studio. He'd filled this writing space with various things that sparked his creative energy, yet he wasn't achieving his ambition as quickly as he'd hoped. In fact, he was struggling to even make it down the garden to start.

Malcolm was trying to do this alongside his demanding, full-time medical career. As we worked together, he identified that he needed something to strengthen the basic belief that he could be both a doctor and a writer. Through discussion we developed a routine that he could experiment with. This daily routine would incorporate a mantra – 'I am a writer' – to help him get writing.

His routine was as follows:

- 6 a.m. rise on a work day.

- Series of yoga stretches while repeating the mantra 'I am a writer.'

- Walking with a cup of coffee to the studio.

- 'Free writing' for five minutes.

- One hour of writing the book.

- Leave for work.

The deliberate daily attention Malcolm paid to this routine proved the spark for his writing. He says it 'moved me from not writing at all to having many new chapters in draft. It was the routine I needed to get me started again, and I still use it now when the studio seems so dark, cold and far away.'

So Malcolm's new skill was to define a daily routine and make it habitual. Another client, Vanessa, chose to focus on the new skill of 'reframing' – telling herself a more useful story.

Returning from a TED-style conference in Spain where she'd been asked to speak, Vanessa sent me this text:

Well, I survived it! Presentation went well and got good feedback. Q&A was a disaster which I'll tell you about when I see you.

When we met, she told me she had been hoping this talk would be a springboard for her long-term ambition to become an expert speaker on building multi-platform businesses. The presentation had gone well in front of an influential audience and then came 'that question'. It seemed to have little relevance to her presentation and consequently she couldn't think of an immediate answer. Instead, she shrugged, grimaced and said nothing. She described it as 'a very long and awkward pause where I felt and looked stupid – I couldn't respond with any intelligent answer.'

This moment haunted her for the next forty-eight hours.

She told me: 'I can't remember a single conversation from the dinner that evening. I just kept turning "the moment when I couldn't answer" over and over in my mind and felt such a fool. I slept really badly and, even on the plane home, found myself reviewing it over and over.'

That was her assessment of her own performance. I asked if she'd received feedback from anyone else. She replied – as if it was somehow an irrelevant question – that her colleagues in the London office had told her that, on social media, people at the conference had been saying how brilliant she'd been. One audience member had tweeted: 'Just witnessed a short masterclass in multi-platform business strategy.' She hadn't mentioned that.

By choosing to focus on one moment in the way she did, Vanessa had drained her energy to connect with others over dinner, given herself a poor night's sleep, ruined her return journey and, more importantly, begun to feel as if her long-term goal was disappearing further into the distance.

I asked what skill she thought would help bring it closer again. She said she really wanted to be a lot better at noticing what was working for her as a speaker. 'Why had I chosen not to see that speech as a masterclass like they had? I just want to tell that story.'

We dug a bit deeper to define the specific skill she was after. I asked, 'What's the first step that'll help you make that better choice: to focus on what is working?'

She paused and said, 'What I'm doing now. This. Pausing.'

This skill – deliberately choosing to pause – is often the first deliberate step that helps people take control of the story they tell themselves. To return them to neutral. To help them reframe it.

> 'We were built to over-learn from negative experiences, but under-learn from positive ones.'
>
> Rick Hanson, psychologist

If Vanessa could let her Human brain pause – just for a bit – it would slow her down enough so she could choose to appreciate that a brief tricky experience is just *one moment* among many positive ones. That way she could have a more balanced reaction, take on any learning and choose a more useful story to help her towards her goal.

> 'Nobody but me is gonna change my story.'
>
> *Matilda: The Musical*

Vanessa immediately felt more in control by deliberately deciding to pay more attention to choosing to pause. It was her first step.

So, holding in mind your long-term goal – to fire your willpower – what is the most useful action, routine or skill to start you off? Here are some examples that others have chosen as their first steps:

Long-Term Goal to Power Will	First-Step Action/Skill/Routine
To set up my own business so I can be autonomous	Gather research
To be in a fulfilling, happy relationship to start a family	Go out and meet more people
To be a strong leader for the success of the company	Run effective and purposeful meetings
To manage a tricky person to benefit team morale	Self-talk mantra to keep me focused

To be a strong presenter so I can motivate others to act	Effective preparation routine
To achieve great A levels so I can study where I choose	Set 90-minute No Distraction slots to focus my revision
To be fit and healthy to keep my job and feel happier	Commit to a regular exercise routine
To be a professional singer so I can make a living from what I love	Diaphragmatic breathing
To be a better dad so my children have a strong role model	Spend more time with my kids
To sleep more so I can wake up feeling positive	Create downtime to switch off

3. What and how are you going to practise?

'I fear not the man who has practised a thousand kicks. I fear the man who has practised one kick a thousand times.'

Bruce Lee

Having prioritized your first step towards your long-term goal, it's time to decide what practice you will regularly undertake to make that a reality. As *The Cambridge Handbook* says, 'You will need to invest that time wisely, by engaging in "deliberate" practice – practice that focuses on tasks beyond your current level of competence and comfort.'

According to the saying, practice makes perfect. Actually, a more accurate statement is: practice makes permanent. Practice of any kind is the hard work of repetition. Done enough, it turns any new behaviour into a habit because the human brain is excellent at remembering patterns. You build a habit if you commit to a practice and repeat it. And repeat it. And repea— you get the idea.

The question is: is it the most useful practice?

It's the quality of what you are practising that matters. I know many organizations that repeatedly hold meetings, but that 'practice' is by no means a measurement of how effective those meetings are. Driving for many years doesn't mean we become better drivers. My mum had been driving for over thirty years when she was stopped attempting to go *over* a roundabout. Being deliberate about *what* you are practising and *how* you are practising shortens the journey to becoming better.

We need to develop deliberate ways to override our less useful habits with more useful ones. *Override* is the key term here. We can't ever get rid of our less useful habits – if only we could – and using self-control to try to avoid them saps our energy. Instead we have to develop more useful ones that are stronger. Habits and routines reduce the need for self-control and conserve our energy.

But cultivating new habits is not easy. An established habit is like a well-worn country path across a meadow that people have followed for years and trodden down. As a new walker arriving at the meadow we tread it too, thankful it's there. No need to think about which way to go – we can just enjoy it. If we choose to walk across by a different route, it will require more thought, more effort, more forceful strides to create a new path. The old path will always be available though, tempting us with the easier alternative. Especially when you're rushing. The second time we take this new path it'll still require effort. Less than the first time, but still more than taking the original path. Likewise, the third attempt requires less effort than the second, and so on. The important thing is to practise pausing to override and resist the short-term temptations our Dog and Reptile brains push for. Be deliberate – however tempting and simple the alternative is.

Nadiya Hussain, the 2015 winner of *The Great British Bake-Off*, had put on three stone after the birth of her third child. She knew that this was mainly due to her mother's delicious curries – her mother would show her love through cooking not one, or even three, but *six* curries a day. Nadiya determined to lose the weight and embarked on a fitness regime, running ten miles a day for three months. She also knew that creating distance between her and the habitual temptation of those lovely curries was vital if she was to accomplish that goal and, painful though it was, she didn't visit her mother in all that time.

As Baumeister says, 'Habitual behaviour runs on automatic pilot . . . you need to override the automatic pilot and take charge with deliberate control.'

Recently I was driving to see a client and thinking about our pending interaction. My Dog brain, recognizing a familiar junction, said, *You're thinking about other stuff. I remember this route, leave it with me,* and took control. Before I knew it, I found myself driving in completely the wrong direction and halfway to the school where I had worked over fifteen years ago. A well-embedded old habit (my automatic pilot) had taken over.

Old patterns of behaviour take real effort to override. And if we're preoccupied or tired, it's even harder. But, to become better at anything, we have to apply our mind energy to let the Human brain do what it does best – make a deliberate choice.

A drill is a way of making practice more effective. The more specific the drill, the easier it is to put it into action and learn from it. Drills are most effective if you are disciplined about doing the specific practice at a certain time and in a certain way.

In an experiment conducted by S. E. Milne, S. Orbell and P. Sheeran in 1999, a group of participants was asked to commit to exercise once a week. A second group was asked to exercise once a week and was given detailed information about how exercise substantially reduces the risk of heart disease. A third group was asked to commit to exercising once a week at a specific time, on a specific day, in a specific location. In the first group, 29 per cent completed the set task. In group 2, 39 per cent did. In the third group that figure more than doubled to 91 per cent.

Creating a drill where you don't have to think about when, how or where you'll execute it, maximizes your mind energy and enables your new habit to be adopted faster. Try to attach the trigger to actions you already do with little effort: every time you walk through the door; whenever you check your emails; in the ten minutes before you go to bed, and so on. If you remember Val and her need to hydrate herself, she found it a very helpful prompt to take a sip of water whenever her phone rang.

Research tells us that, for any deliberate quality practice to become a habit, it needs to be repeated many times in a disciplined way. The US Marines estimate that muscle memory takes 300 repetitions and muscle mastery 3,000. Babies don't count the amount of repetitions they do when it comes to learning to walk. The skill is to stand up and put one foot in front of the other – with the aid of chair legs, sideboards and grandparents. They fall over a lot during their practice. It doesn't matter to them. Their long-term goal – to do what everyone around them is doing – is strong enough to help them persevere with the drill until eventually, voila! They are up and halfway to the kitchen. This method is universally known as trial and error. Perhaps it ought to be trial and correct. In fact, we call it act and learn. Little people try to walk, fall over, learn from it, get up, and try again – all powered by a strong will to be like everyone else. Watching a baby go through this practice is the embodiment of what Samuel Beckett wrote in *Worstward Ho* (1983):

Ever tried. Ever failed. No matter. Try again. Fail again. Fail better.

Mind drills (mantras) are hugely useful. The mantras

we're taught at school remain with us as adults, for instance, '*i* before *e*, except after *c*' – maybe because they rhyme but mostly because they were drilled into us.

Our daughter was having trouble in Year 1 remembering which *w* words had an *h* in them and which didn't. She couldn't get her head around why the letter should be in there if you couldn't hear it in the word. So we developed a mantra that we all sang every day on the way to primary school. It went like this (it needs a beat to make it really work!):

> When, what, which,
> Why, where, who,
> They have an *h*
> After *w*.

She remembers it to this day – and so do we.

The mind mantra is used in sport a lot. Many athletes use mantras at different points in a race. Ryan Vail, the American marathon runner with a personal best of two hours, ten minutes, regularly says, 'One more mile.'

Drilling a mantra has a boosting effect – *as long as* it's positive and useful. Telling yourself you feel like crap is, to some extent, a self-fulfilling prophecy. An internal dialogue isn't just a response to how you feel; it shapes how you feel. Both times I was in labour, my mantra of 'One contraction closer to meeting my baby' helped me through the pain of childbirth.

Once you've chosen your practice – whether it's body, mood or mind – drilling it requires your mind energy.

Deliberately drill it until it becomes automatic, or, as one client put it, 'until it is baked in'.

It goes without saying that your drill will be specific to the skill you have identified for your 'be better' journey. However, in case you're looking for inspiration, here are examples from some other people's journeys.

Long-Term Goal to Power Will	First-Step Action/ Skill/Routine	Drill to Practise
To set up my own business so I can be autonomous	Gather research	An hour every day focused on gathering one useful fact
To be in a fulfilling, happy relationship to start a family	Go out and meet more people	Say yes to every social event offered and actively create one a week
To be a strong leader for the success of the company	Run effective and purposeful meetings	Put 2 hours in diary to prep agenda 3 days before, with clear outputs for each item
To manage a tricky person to benefit team morale	Self-talk mantra to keep me focused	Deliberate mantra every time I meet him: 'Stay calm – he's great at the detail'
To be a strong presenter so I can motivate others to act	Effective preparation routine	Rigorous plan in diary: create content (X hours); rehearsal (X hours)

To achieve great A levels so I can study where I choose	Set 90-minute No Distraction slots to focus my revision	Use an alarm to start and finish every session
To be fit and healthy to keep my job and feel happier	Commit to a regular exercise routine	5-minute exercise routine before my shower every morning
To be a professional singer so I can make a living from what I love	Diaphragmatic breathing	Set 'breathing alarm' on my phone 4 times a day. Repeat breathing exercise 6 times at each alarm
To be a better dad so my children have a strong role model	Spend more time with my kids	3 work-free early evenings every week
To sleep more so I can wake up feeling positive	Create downtime to switch off	Turn off all devices at 9 p.m.

4. Who can best support you?

One last visit to *The Cambridge Handbook*:

> You will need a well-informed coach not only to guide you through deliberate practice but also to help you learn how to coach yourself.

Making changes to how we choose to be or what we choose to do is not easy on our own. Any deliberate practice is helped when we can learn with someone alongside to support, encourage and guide us.

The *Handbook* goes on to describe high performers as open to, curious about and even craving feedback – as long as they think it might help them be better. As quoted earlier, the *Handbook* also says your will has to be strong enough to take 'painful assessment' from both yourself and others. Many of us think we're capable of doing quality practice alone when we aren't. A knowledgeable, challenging *and* supportive coach/teacher/mentor is crucial. I would've had no idea, for example, about the exaggerated turnout on my right foot – a hangover from years of ballet – and its impact on my knee when I exercise, without the expert help of Luke, my (very patient) personal trainer.

I actively invite clients to choose a couple of people who can give them encouragement and feedback – I call them Phil & Jill. Clients often find the modern perception of a court jester a useful analogy for this role. A person who witnesses you – sometimes close up, sometimes from afar – and is happy to tell you the truth, hold you to account, cheer you on and offer advice. A useful companion on your journey to your goal. The outside eye to help you keep practising and learning as you go.

Amir was helped to improve by his Phil – and it wasn't human!

Amir was becoming more and more frustrated with a member of his team who just wasn't producing the quality of work he wanted. He described this person as 'closed' and 'increasingly defensive' every time they had a conversation. We worked together on planning the next conversation and I suggested coming in to observe him.

Many clients find 'real time' observation the most useful way to identify the skill they want to get better at. Filming it and then sitting together to play the film back and analyse it often helps a client identify a behaviour of which they were completely unaware – both useful and less useful. After some initial reticence, Amir agreed that it could be helpful, both in helping him to get better at asking questions – the skill he wanted to focus on – and in demonstrating that he was up for learning too. So I filmed the conversation.

Afterwards I asked Amir how successful he felt he'd been in achieving his aim. How would he score himself out of 10?

He said, 'I think I did OK actually. I'd give myself a 6.'

I asked what he thought he'd done that was most useful.

He replied, 'I was consciously asking more questions and slowing down any immediate reactions I had.'

I agreed. I had noticed him consciously doing that. I asked, 'What could you have done to be more useful in the meeting? To lift your score to, say, a 7?'

He was less clear about that. 'Perhaps I could've asked a few more questions. What score would you have given me?'

I told Amir I would give him a 4. He was clearly put out. We then watched the footage and I asked him to rate himself again.

He nodded. 'Ah, OK, I get it. I misjudged myself completely. I looked disinterested when he was answering. I glanced over towards the window – only for a short time, but I can see why that might've been off-putting. I didn't realize I did that. Also, when he answered my second question . . . what was my face doing? I looked irritated before he'd even finished answering. I asked good questions but I could've been a lot better at listening to his replies.'

Thanks to opening himself up to feedback around this experience, Amir identified a different skill: to listen with more genuine curiosity. From the footage, he identified a few things he could do with his body to help him remain more present and genuinely curious. He had a few behavioural patterns he could pay more attention to over the coming weeks. All thanks to his Phil, the camera. This agenda-free feedback simply showed him what he did. That's why it's a primary learning tool within the worlds of sport and the performing arts, and in teaching, too. I encourage most clients to use it. Most initially hate the idea, but they ultimately find it invaluable.

I asked Amir to identify someone internally who could continue this kind of open, honest and possibly painful feedback. He asked another team member to take up the role. This person was a straight talker and had previously offered him feedback about his 'abruptness'. Amir invited her to play an active part in helping him develop this skill and tell him how he had done after each meeting.

Amir was proactively asking for feedback, and it

gradually became a key part of how the team worked together. He'd put himself up for modelling the idea of using a Phil & Jill to learn and improve. Now others were doing the same. A few months later, he told me, 'It was a bit painful being filmed, but I learnt that I wasn't listening the way I thought. Good news is I've discovered I'm trainable. If I hadn't done that I'd never have known I could look so disinterested. I now pay attention to how I listen. He and I have a better working relationship, which has had a positive impact on the quality of his work.'

You can also have a useful Phil & Jill within your own family. I received some unasked-for feedback – from my son. In the middle of a heated discussion over a decision he was making that I thought was wrong, he said, 'Mum, I need you to get off my wing.' It was a moment of realization: time to step back as a parent and allow him, a growing teenager, to step into his independence. I had to reboot what being a useful mum meant. It was a new skill, and it needed some deliberate practice. I knew he would be a very useful Phil. Irritating, but useful.

Actually, now I think of it, both my children deal in unasked-for feedback. One evening, as I was asking my daughter – for the third or fourth time that day – to *please* tidy her room, she erupted. 'I HAVE, Mum! Why is it you only focus on the bits that are messy and never see the bits I've already cleared?' Another wake-up call. I regularly ask clients to focus on what is working as much as possible to get the best from themselves and others. Here I was doing the exact opposite. I hadn't chosen that. My Dog brain had chosen for me.

Of course, having established your skill and your drill, you could decide to self-assess. But it's risky. Self-assessment can be highly unreliable. Ernest Hemingway used to track his daily word output on a chart, 'so as not to kid myself'. Considering this was before the days of the automatic word count, that is pretty painstaking.

If you can be honest enough to give yourself the 'painful assessment' you may need, then feel free. Be your own Phil & Jill. As a start, try these feedback questions that I offer to my clients so they can assess, not guess:

1. How useful is your practice in helping you achieve your goal?

2. What is useful about that practice?

3. What would make the practice more useful?

(And strictly speaking, as I'm asking these questions, I'm now your Phil & Jill.)

Whatever skill you've deliberately decided to drill, it is an important step forward to identify and recruit your Phil & Jill. Clients often find it useful to give them different roles. For example, one to cheer you on and increase your confidence to keep going. The other who knows what the 'better' you're after looks like and can help you act and learn. An expert in your eyes. One client recently described this type of Phil & Jill as 'someone who's already seen the film'.

Our Phil & Jills can help us become better in different ways. Below are some examples:

Long-Term Goal to Power Will	First-Step Action/Skill/Routine	Drill to Practise	Phil & Jill Support
To set up my own business so I can be autonomous	Gather research	An hour every day focused on gathering one useful fact	A successful business owner as mentor
To be in a fulfilling, happy relationship to start a family	Go out and meet more people	Say yes to every social event offered and actively create one a week	My flatmate & an 'outgoing' aunt
To be a strong leader for the success of the company	Run effective and purposeful meetings	Put 2 hours in diary to prep agenda 3 days before, with clear outputs for each item	A key colleague in the team & my boss
To manage a tricky person to benefit team morale	Self-talk mantra to keep me focused	Deliberate mantra every time I meet him: 'Stay calm – he's great at the detail'	The tricky person & my PA
To be a strong presenter so I can motivate others to act	Effective preparation routine	Rigorous plan in diary: create content (X hours); rehearsal (X hours)	My performance coach + camera (me on film!)

To achieve great A levels so I can study where I choose	Set 90-minute No Distraction slots to focus my revision	Use an alarm to start and finish every session	My teacher & my mum
To be fit and healthy to keep my job and feel happier	Commit to a regular exercise routine	5-minute exercise routine before my shower every morning	My husband & my Fitbit group
To be a professional singer so I can make a living from what I love	Diaphragmatic breathing	Set 'breathing alarm' on my phone 4 times a day. Repeat breathing exercise 6 times at each alarm	My singing coach & recording myself
To be a better dad so my children have a strong role model	Spend more time with my kids	3 work-free early evenings every week	My PA & my kids
To sleep more so I can wake up feeling positive	Create downtime to switch off	Turn off all devices at 9 p.m.	My girlfriend & a sleep app

Let's pause for a moment and take a look at what you have covered so far.

PAUSE

Hopefully, by now, you are clearer about what you want to be better at and why it matters to you; what specific action is going to set you on your way; how you're going to practise it and who is going to support you en route.

That could be enough to help focus your mind energy on deliberately building the new habit.

Here are three more questions that others find help embed it and increase their motivation to keep going.

5. How can you make it fun?

I'd like to mash together two old adages: 'We don't stop playing because we grow old, we grow old because we stop playing' and 'You can't teach an old dog new tricks.'

Here goes:

Whatever age you are, keep playing and you can always learn.

Maybe not quite as catchy, but I wholeheartedly believe you can learn at *any* age, and learning anything is easier when the learning is fun.

Focusing on whether what you are doing is right or wrong is one way of learning, and one I come across a lot – both in individuals learning and in organizations. It can work, but it's not the only way to learn. The pressure of getting something right or wrong can immobilize people. It can stop them making progress or even wanting to try. There is another way: a less structured, more play-ful, curiosity-driven way of learning that is equally beneficial. I know that a lot of the students I taught would stick with the experiment of getting better at something for longer if the learning had an element of fun in it. As one student told me, 'I like doing this, miss. Doesn't feel like hard work. It feels chilled.'

An American tennis pro by the name of Timothy Gall-wey had a great way of making his students see tennis lessons as 'chilled'. He saw them make faster progress when they tried less. There is old film footage of him undergoing a challenge – to coach a class of students, none of whom would call themselves sportsmen or sportswomen. Indeed, some had never held a racket before. He was given ten minutes to teach them tennis. He said in the film, 'The idea is to just let the body do what it is capable of doing. That's hard because the mind is saying, "I want to do better. I want to do better. I want to get this ball over the net."'

He noticed that they excelled at getting in their own way. They placed pressure on themselves by trying to get their feet in the *right* position before hitting the ball or trying hard to hit the ball with the *right* part of the racket. He asked them instead to just watch the ball. In fact, he actually said (and the language is important), 'All you have to do is watch the ball.' The Dog brain is already hearing, *All I have to do* . . . Sounds easy. The instant the students saw the ball hit the ground, they were to shout, 'Bounce!' And as they saw the ball hit the racket, they had to shout, 'Hit!' That was all they were to focus on.

When they tried serving, he asked them to hum, placing the emphasis on hearing the rhythm of the hum to execute the serve rather than on any commands. He wanted them 'to focus the mind's attention so it won't interfere with the body's ability to hit the ball automatically. Not focusing on trying to hit it, just hitting it. Put the mind somewhere where it can stay calm, relaxed and interested, then the body does it beautifully.'

Humans learn best when they play – making an exercise not seem like an exercise; making a drill not feel like a drill; making the challenge chilled and achievable.

One of my clients had a seven-year-old daughter who was becoming anxious at school. So her mum created 'Where to?' days with her daughter at the weekends. They would drive off in the car and, at each junction or roundabout, would take it in turns to decide which way to turn. They didn't consult any maps or the sat-nav until they decided to head home. She had created a light way for her daughter to have fun and feel safe around not knowing.

An extraordinary example is the work of a social enterprise in the UK called Breathe Arts Health Research. They started a project called Breathe Magic to help children with hemiplegia, a neurological condition that means the patients have varying degrees of weakness, stiffness and lack of control in the limbs of one or other side of their body.

What would normally be described as an exercise is reframed as a magic trick. Every trick requires the children to practise precise movements that, unbeknown to them, incorporate the rehabilitation exercises that therapists would ask them to do to improve their hand and arm function. These include classic tricks like the 'cup and ball', which requires them to turn over a cup in their hand and use their thumb and forefinger to pick up the ball. These actions develop essential movements like forearm rotation, grasp, release and coordination. Equally, tricks with pieces of rope incorporate movements to develop stretching and dexterity. They also develop the children into little magicians.

And the joy of it is that these tricks need plenty of repetition if the children are to perfect them. The repetitive nature of practising magic tricks helps build up the children's strength and dexterity in their weaker hand/arm. After they finish the programme, the children can often carry out daily living activities for the first time in their lives – activities like getting dressed independently or cutting up their own food. The result has been a 50 per cent reduction in the time the parents and carers report that they need to support their child (almost four hours a day). And the children think they've been practising magic. That's the real magic.

So, how can you keep your learning fun and chilled? Here are some ways others do it:

Long-Term Goal to Power Will	First-Step Action/ Skill/ Routine	Drill to Practise	Phil & Jill Support	Fun and Chilled Learning
To set up my own business so I can be autonomous	Gather research	An hour every day focused on gathering one useful fact	A successful business owner as mentor	Have a cup of tea and play a memory game to recall the top 5 tips of the week

To be in a fulfilling, happy relationship to start a family	Go out and meet more people	Say yes to every social event offered and actively create one a week	My flatmate & an 'outgoing' aunt	Have my flatmate place 'SAY YES!' Post-its in different places to surprise me
To be a strong leader for the success of the company	Run effective and purposeful meetings	Put 2 hours in diary to prep agenda 3 days before, with clear outputs for each item	A key colleague in the team & my boss	Anyone can show me a 'yellow card' if they feel I could be clearer in a meeting
To manage a tricky person to benefit team morale	Self-talk mantra to keep me focused	Deliberate mantra every time I meet him: 'Stay calm – he's great at the detail'	The tricky person & my PA	Laugh with friends at moments when I could have done it better
To be a strong presenter so I can motivate others to act	Effective preparation routine	Rigorous plan in diary: create content (X hours); rehearsal (X hours)	My perform-ance coach + camera (me on film!)	Get my 6-year-old daughter to sit on my notes while I say my speech out loud

To achieve great A levels so I can study where I choose	Set 90-minute No Distraction slots to focus my revision	Use an alarm to start and finish every session	My teacher & my mum	Create cheeky, fun mnemonics with friends to help remember the dry stuff
To be fit and healthy to keep my job and feel happier	Commit to a regular exercise routine	5-minute exercise routine before my shower every morning	My husband & my Fitbit group	Each week my husband creates a playlist of two favourite songs for me to exercise to
To be a professional singer so I can make a living from what I love	Diaphragmatic breathing	Set 'breathing alarm' on my phone 4 times a day. Repeat breathing exercise 6 times at each alarm	My singing coach & recording myself	I walk across the park and do my 'pant' breathing in time with my steps
To be a better dad so my children have a strong role model	Spend more time with my kids	3 work-free early evenings every week	My PA & my kids	At leaving time, my PA emails, 'YOU HAVE JUST LEFT THE BUILD-ING!'

To sleep more so I can wake up feeling positive	Create downtime to switch off	Turn off all devices at 9 p.m.	My girlfriend & a sleep app	Form a WhatsApp group to share tips & laughs

6. How will you stop and reflect?

Mind energy benefits from frequent breaks. It is hard, and often unproductive, to try to sustain concentrated effort for too long. It's pointless trying to force-feed yourself with too much information at once. The brain will simply stop receiving. We need time to process.

Ernest Hemingway would walk away when his writing wasn't going well, precisely to give himself a break. A break from 'the awful responsibility of writing', or, as he sometimes called it, 'the responsibility of awful writing'.

I witness many people forcing themselves to keep going, to 'crack on' through the many things they have to do when it might be more useful to take a stillness break: a moment to reconnect to their long-term goal and digest any learning. Sometimes, when I work with a group, I ask them to just stop and take five minutes to be still and consider what's important about what they've been discussing, learning or rehearsing. I like to describe this break as 'inside time'. To just enjoy the opportunity to stop and be. For some, the discomfort of being still and quiet is palpable. The urges and impulses kick in, pushing them to reach for their devices and feel like they're achieving. Doing.

Have you ever approached a queue of traffic on the motorway and decided to take the next exit even though you're not exactly sure where it will lead you? My husband calls this 'a long cut'. It may take us miles off course and make our journey longer by half an hour but it satisfies our sense of achievement more than just sitting still in the traffic. It's another Dog brain impulse.

How can we be more deliberate in creating and using moments of stillness? The pause space allows the three brains to reorganize and realign through a moment of reflection. It can help us work at our best, yet we're too often compelled to keep going regardless – to keep doing. Stopping – even for five minutes – to reflect on what we're doing and how we're doing it can help us assess whether it's the most useful thing to continue to do. It can even help us to go faster – if that's what we want. Going slow to go fast.

When we moved into our current house, we employed a builder who we regularly spotted sitting on a box, paint pot or breezeblock, sucking on a mint and staring randomly into space – in other words, not working. Finally, I built up the courage – during one of these breaks – to ask if there was anything I could do to speed up the process of completion as Christmas was fast approaching. He looked up, clearly sensed my anxiety, raised a hand and said, 'Don't worry. This is my Polo moment.'

That 'Polo moment', it turns out, was essential for him to complete the work in the best, most efficient way. While I thought he was wasting time, he was actually taking time – the time it takes to suck a Polo – to step back from the project and assess everything he needed to do to get the job done. A 'Polo moment' is another phrase that's now part of our household vocabulary. And yes, the house was finished by Christmas.

I have many clients who've identified an environment where they can usefully be still. It might be a cafe they like, a view they love, a park bench. They take some time out purposefully to be still and reflect on what and how they're doing in relation to what they want to be better at. The environment makes a useful difference, acting as a trigger to be still. So, as you pause, take a moment to read what others do in their still time.

Long-term Goal to Power Will	First-Step Action/Skill/Routine	Drill to Practise	Phil&Jill Support	Fun and Chilled Learning	Stillness to Reflect
To set up my own business so I can be autonomous	Gather research	An hour every day focused on gathering one useful fact	A successful business owner as mentor	Have a cup of tea and play a memory game to recall the top 5 tips of the week	I picture the business owner I want to be and assess how close I am in a progress notebook
To be in a fulfilling, happy relationship to start a family	Go out and meet more people	Say yes to every social event offered and actively create one a week	My flatmate & an 'outgoing' aunt	Have my flatmate place 'SAY YES!' Post-its in different places to surprise me	In my favourite cafe, I enjoy writing in a notebook the useful comments others have made about my confidence

To be a strong leader for the success of the company	Run effective and purposeful meetings	Put 2 hours in diary to prep agenda 3 days before, with clear outputs for each item	A key colleague in the team & my boss	Anyone can show me a 'yellow card' if they feel I could be clearer in a meeting	Once a week, deliberately stop and ask two questions: what have I learnt? What one thing can I improve?
To manage a tricky person to benefit team morale	Self-talk mantra to keep me focused	Deliberate mantra every time I meet him: 'Stay calm – he's great at the detail'	The tricky person & my PA	Laugh with friends at moments when I could have done it better	In the park, I consciously focus on the interactions that went better this week
To be a strong presenter so I can motivate others to act	Effective preparation routine	Rigorous plan in diary: create content (X hours); rehearsal (X hours)	My performance coach & camera (me on film!)	Get my 6-year-old daughter to sit on my notes while I say my speech out loud	After rehearsals I watch the footage and consider what works and what needs work

To achieve great A levels so I can study where I choose	Set 90-minute No Distraction slots to focus my revision	Use an alarm to start and finish every session	My teacher & my mum	Create cheeky, fun mnemonics with friends to help remember the dry stuff	I've joined a yoga class. No devices allowed! The quiet allows me to clear my head
To be fit and healthy to keep my job and feel happier	Commit to a regular exercise routine	5-minute exercise routine before my shower every morning	My husband & my Fitbit group	Each week my husband creates a playlist of two favourite songs to exercise to	I have some trousers I want to fit into again. I put them on to see how close I am
To be a professional singer so I can make a living from what I love	Diaphragmatic breathing	Set 'breathing alarm' on my phone 4 times a day. Repeat breathing exercise 6 times at each alarm	My singing coach & recording myself	I walk across the park and do my 'pant' breathing in time with my steps	I look at a photo of the stage I want to sing on and decide on the most useful change for my next breathing practice

To be a better dad so my children have a strong role model	Spend more time with my kids	3 work-free early evenings every week	My PA & my kids	At leaving time, my PA emails, 'YOU HAVE JUST LEFT THE BUILDING!'	I remember the joy I had with my dad and savour that child–father connection
To sleep more so I can wake up feeling positive	Create downtime to switch off	Turn off all devices at 9 p.m.	My girlfriend & a sleep app	Form a WhatsApp group to share tips and laughs	It helps just to be still. The more I connect with that feeling, the better sleeper I will be

7. How will you celebrate?

Recognizing effort and the thrill of progress is an important ingredient in becoming better. Each celebration recharges the will and motivation. These moments drive us forward and help us to maintain confidence in the effort we are putting in, increasing the chances of us wanting to do it again. It's the principle behind things like children's star charts and achieving the next level in video games. I am currently learning French via an app, and I am constantly buoyed by fanfares of achievement as I complete a 'lesson'.

Giving ourselves a proverbial pat on the back before moving forward feels good and reminds us that we are in control and can do something different. Sometimes the key role I play with a client who's building a new habit is helping them notice the effort they're putting in and the progress they're making – progress they might otherwise ignore in their determination to keep striving. It's a resource that we can all use to help us recharge. Ignore it and we might miss that opportunity to feel the thrill and to be better at it sooner.

When we have a planned way of celebrating, it acts as a powerful incentive to keep going. As we've already decided when we're going to celebrate, we are conserving our mind energy too – like Barack Obama with his suits. I know that having the star chart on the fridge for our children – with the celebration moment in bright colours at the end of the week, screaming, *Look. You'll have this when you've stuck to it!* – was a massive incentive to keep going. I notice that, as adults, we could do with paying more attention to marking moments of achievement.

One client had set herself the target of losing weight. She identified a particular leather jacket that she would buy herself when she hit her target weight. It became a powerful incentive. She drew a six-week timeline on her kitchen wall and placed a picture of the jacket alongside her target weight. Every time she successfully completed a week towards her goal, she moved the picture a week on. That moment of moving it closer – seeing the weeks and her weight reduce – became an important mark of celebration.

Most organizations could be better at it too. I sometimes sense a reticence – that it runs the risk of being an unhelpful distraction from the 'real work'. I hear comments like 'If we celebrate, we might send the message out that everyone can relax. We don't want that', or 'I want them to focus on the problem and sort it out, not waste time celebrating.' I hear parents say, 'I'm not going to tell them it's good – they might stop trying.' Obviously, you will choose whether or not to do it, but in the high-performance worlds that I know of, they choose to pay attention to their achievements.

How might you do that as you get better?

Here are some examples of how others do it:

Long-Term Goal to Power Will	First-Step Action/Skill/ Routine	Drill to Practise	Phil & Jill Support	Fun and Chilled Learning	Stillness to Reflect	Thrill of Progress
To set up my own business so I can be autonomous	Gather research	An hour every day focused on gathering one useful fact	A successful business owner as mentor	Have a cup of tea and play a memory game to recall the top 5 tips of the week	I picture the business owner I want to be and assess how close I am in a progress notebook	Arrange a game of football with my mates

To be in a fulfilling, happy relationship to start a family	Go out and meet more people	Say yes to every social event offered and actively create one a week	My flatmate & an 'outgoing' aunt	Have my flatmate place 'SAY YES!' Post-its in different places to surprise me	In my favourite cafe, I enjoy capturing useful comments others have made about my confidence	Go on a shopping spree and buy something nice with a friend
To be a strong leader for the success of the company	Run effective and purposeful meetings	Put 2 hours in diary to prep agenda 3 days before, with clear outputs for each item	A key colleague in the team & my boss	Anyone can show me a 'yellow card' if they feel I could be clearer in a meeting	Once a week, deliberately stop and ask two questions: what have I learnt? What one thing can I improve?	Put on my headphones to cut out the busy-ness and listen to my favourite playlist

To manage a tricky person to benefit team morale	Self-talk mantra to keep me focused	Deliberate mantra every time I meet him: 'Stay calm – he's great at the detail'	The tricky person & my PA	Laugh with friends at moments when I could have done it better	In the park, I consciously focus on the interactions that went better this week	If I feel I've managed myself better, I treat myself to a glass of wine
To be a strong presenter so I can motivate others to act	Effective preparation routine	Rigorous plan in diary: create content (X hours); rehearsal (X hours)	My performance coach + camera (me on film!)	Get my 6-year-old daughter to sit on my notes while I say my speech out loud	After rehearsals, I watch the footage. Consider what works and what needs work	Book a massage
To achieve great A levels so I can study where I choose	Set 90-minute No Distraction slots to focus my revision	Use an alarm to start and finish every session	My teacher & my mum	Create cheeky, fun mnemonics with friends to help remember the dry stuff	I've joined a yoga class. No devices allowed! The quiet allows me to clear my head	Get out to a party – there's always one to go to

To be fit and healthy to keep my job and feel happier	Commit to a regular exercise routine	5-minute exercise routine before my shower every morning	My husband and my Fitbit group	Each week my husband creates a playlist of two favourite songs to exercise to	I have some trousers I want to fit into again. I put them on to see how close I am	If the trousers are less tight, I put £5 in a jar towards a new pair – in that size!
To be a professional singer so I can make a living from what I love	Diaphragmatic breathing	Set 'breathing alarm' on my phone 4 times a day. Repeat breathing exercise 6 times at each alarm	My singing coach & recording myself	I walk across the park and do my 'pant' breathing in time with my steps	I look at a photo of the stage I want to sing on and decide the most useful change for my next breathing practice	Karaoke with mates – always a laugh!

To be a better dad so my children have a strong role model	Spend more time with my kids	3 work-free early evenings every week	My PA & my kids	At leaving time, my PA emails, 'YOU HAVE JUST LEFT THE BUILDING!'	I remember the joy I had with my dad and savour that child–father connection	The biggest reward I get is the run and hug I receive as I walk through the front door
To sleep more so I can wake up feeling positive	Create downtime to switch off	Turn off all devices at 9 p.m.	My girl-friend & a sleep app	Form a WhatsApp group to share tips and laughs	It helps just to be still. The more I connect with that feeling, the better sleeper I will be	An extra 30 minutes of deep sleep means I celebrate with a bacon sandwich

Trying to remember all seven questions every time you want to build a new habit will unnecessarily use up your mind energy. To save you from that, here is a simple, fun and easy aide-memoire to use:

The Habit Rhyme
Will,
Skill, Drill,
Phil & Jill,
Chill, Still and Thrill

SUMMARY

Our mind energy is central to making useful, deliberate choices. Its effectiveness depends, of course, on whether you have your SHED in order. Mind energy is the fuel that fires our brilliant Human brain and is at the heart of building any new habit – be it a body habit, mood habit or mind habit. The more effectively we focus our mind energy, the more likely we are to make better choices and become better at anything.

Our Five Energies

Body Energy

Mood Energy

Mind Energy

Purpose Energy

People Energy

8.

CHOOSE WHY IT MATTERS

'He who has a *why* for life can bear almost any *how*.'

Nietzsche

Purpose energy is fired up when we connect *what* we do to *why* it matters to others. When I witness this energy in clients, they are connecting to something much more profound than just achieving their own goal. The energy is palpable and they come alive. I can feel it. I see the clues in their body, in their eyes, in their tone and in the words they use – phrases like *It's what I'm here to do*; *I'm passionate about it*; *I just knew I had to do it*; *It's my calling.* This is part of its magic. It's the energy of meaning beyond self-interest and it has the potential to galvanize all our other energies to achieve far more than we imagined possible. It imbues our actions with larger meaning. It's the energy behind what I call *soul choices*: to stay awake at a loved one's bedside for days at a time without sleep; to run marathons to raise money for charities; to carry one's entire family onto a crowded, unsafe boat in the hope of creating a better and safer life. It can reignite or sustain our desire to keep going when it could be easier to give up. This is the one energy that can drive us even if our SHED is not in great shape. But only for a limited amount of time. It's like a reserve tank and can fuel us in emergencies.

Just such an example of the power of purpose energy can be found in the story of Australian Daniel Miller, who found himself trapped in a muddy dam beneath his mechanical digger for five hours, steeped in mud up to his nose. He used a mind mantra to keep himself calm and devised a plan to restrict the amount of effort he would expend in calling for help. He raised his mouth above the water level for ten minutes at a time, screaming 'Help!' as loudly as he could, before he went back to nose breathing, resting and then repeating his cries for help. Eventually a neighbour heard him and he was saved. When asked how he had kept going, he replied, 'I'd promised my wife, who lost her mother to cancer as a young girl, that I would not die before her. I was not going to let her, my nine-year-old and four-year-old find me face down in a dam, dead. That was not going to happen. I was determined to make it.'

And he did.

What Daniel's purpose energy allowed him to achieve in that moment of crisis is almost incomprehensible. Through real stories like this, I have grown to understand its immense power. So, rather than try to define this energy further and perhaps constrain its possibilities for you, I want to share some examples and offer a few simple ways to help you power up your own purpose energy.

There are a couple of very well-known apocryphal stories that have purpose energy at their heart. One revolves around President John F. Kennedy's visit to NASA in 1961. He stopped to introduce himself to a cleaner who was mopping the floor. The President asked him what he was doing at NASA, to which the cleaner replied, 'Sir, I'm helping put a man on the moon.' The other concerns three bricklayers working on rebuilding St Paul's Cathedral five years after the Great Fire of London. In disguise, the architect Sir Christopher Wren asked each of them what job he was doing. The first answered, 'I'm cutting stones.' The second replied, 'I'm building a wall.' The third answered, 'I'm building a cathedral.' In some renditions of this story, the third bricklayer is even reported to have said, 'I'm contributing to rebuilding the great City of London.' Regardless of which version is correct, like any great story that stands the test of time, it embodies a meaning that we can all relate to on some level: the principle of connecting what we're doing to a meaning bigger than ourselves, making a difference to others – a purpose beyond self-interest.

Sadly, I can't tell you whether the cleaner mopped NASA's floors better than any previous cleaner or whether the third bricklayer was the most productive. However, I have witnessed the force of this energy through other, more recent, examples.

During a workshop on purpose with some business leaders, one participant jumped to life and shared a story about the caretaker at his daughter's school. It had snowed heavily overnight and, like most of the UK when this kind of weather occurs, daily life ground to a halt. All the local schools announced they would be closed for the day. Except his daughter's. This was open for business as usual. It turned out that their caretaker had heard the weather forecast and had risen painfully early to get out and sweep all the paths clear of snow and ice, making them safe for the children. According to the head teacher's delighted email afterwards, she had asked him why he'd gone to all that effort. The caretaker replied, 'So the children can keep learning and their parents can still go to work.'

When exploring this force with clients, I might ask, 'When can you remember having connected to this energy before?'

This question always takes my ex-Royal Marine business partner, Simon, back to a time when he was based in a jungle camp in Central America. Close to their camp there was a church run by a nun, Sister Mary. Simon and the other Marines had been supporting her work too. Sister Mary was very diligent about keeping a record of progress with the aid of a small camera that she took everywhere with her. Sadly, on one rare trip into the local town, it was stolen.

A month later, there was a twenty-mile race and the prize was a brand-new, state-of-the-art camera. Simon, a keen runner, but out of condition, entered the race with one purpose in mind. He takes up the story:

> About fifteen miles into the race along hot jungle roads, I had pretty much shot my bolt. I was running on empty. I'd been vying for the lead with another guy for the best part of the last five miles and was now pushing my body way beyond its recent training limits. It was getting tougher and tougher and I could feel my pace deserting me. I was sure my rival could sense it. As I staggered on, wondering how much longer I could continue, a car drove up from behind us and, as it came alongside, I saw at the window Sister Mary waving cheerily at me. I felt a sudden surge of energy and my pace quickened immediately. My rival had no response and I pulled away, winning by several minutes and feeling great.

The sense of achievement in winning the race paled into insignificance alongside that of being able to hand over the camera.

I became aware of the force of this energy in many of the young people I worked with when I was a teacher.

Take Lily, for example. She was never once late for school, always handed her work in on time and was intolerant of some of her classmates' bad behaviour. Some might say she was a model student. As I spent more time with Lily, I learnt that she was the oldest of three and her mother was a drug addict. Every day Lily would get up at 6 a.m., make her younger brother and sister breakfast, walk them to their school and get here early to complete her homework. In one of our conversations I asked her what kept her going. She said, 'My brother and sister need me. They rely on me. I want to be the mum to them that my mum can't.' She was fifteen.

Some people develop their purpose early – and stick with it all their life.

My aunt Agnes knew she wanted to be a nurse from a very young age. Her career followed that path, and she travelled the world as a nurse during the war and then worked as a ward sister until her retirement. Even at the age of eighty-nine, despite a bad hip, arthritic hands and very poor eyesight, she was walking up and down the stairs of her house regularly with a tray of food or a cup of tea for her ailing, bedridden older sister, Jenny. When Jenny died, it was no coincidence that Agnes moved downstairs as the stairs became 'too much for her'. Her purpose was gone.

Purpose energy deferred my aunt's immobility and it can, in some cases, even help delay mortality.

In the 1990s in the north-west US, a doctor diagnosed a woman with an illness that meant she had six months left to live. When she was driving home, she thought about her young children and determined that she would live to see her daughter grow up and graduate from college. This gave what was left of her life focus and purpose. She said that it was that purpose that kept her alive and gave her the energy to get up every morning. She said she lived not for her illness but for her daughter. And she was recounting this some fourteen *years* after that doctor's original prognosis.

Most of us have different purposes at different stages in life.

One client, Stephanie – now in her fifties – was lacking motivation in a job she loved. She was part of a global educational project. It was her passion and had been for a long time. However, as the main spokesperson she was increasingly being asked to speak at events which she didn't enjoy. She hated being in the spotlight. 'I have suddenly become really uncomfortable with this whole Cult of Me thing! I find myself going through the motions. Maybe I've just been doing it too long.'

As I listened, it seemed she was convincing herself that perhaps – at her age – there were other, more youthful, useful voices to hear from. I got a sense she was talking herself out of the role, and was happy to quietly disappear.

I asked her to tell me about the project. As she talked, the telltale signs of purpose energy emerged. Her eyes lit up; she came to life.

I asked her, 'As you talk to me now, what's going on?'

Stephanie reflected, looked away and then spoke – with an emphasis I hadn't heard before.

'I'm talking in service to the *cause* . . . rather than thinking about *me*.' She smiled. 'That already frees me up. Actually, I'm thinking now, I owe it to fifty-plus women to be out there and be onstage. So, I will keep doing them.'

In that two-hour session, I witnessed her move from switched off to switched on by connecting to the power of purpose beyond self.

There are lots of other examples throughout business where people are driven by a purpose that is beyond self-interest. Some organizations tap into this energy through their values or their mission.

I watched a sales team in a global pharmaceutical company becoming completely reignited after seeing and hearing patients talk about the life-enhancing effects of their products. In a session we had afterwards, one member of the team told me, 'I'd been counting down the days to early retirement. Now I've told my husband to hold off on the travel plans. I've changed my mind and intend to work for another five years. What's more I'm going to put myself up for a leadership role.'

I asked her what had happened. She described it like this: 'I saw myself as just another member of the sales team. I now see myself as making a difference to patients' lives.' She had chosen a label to connect her to what really mattered – a purpose label.

When groups of people connect to a collective purpose

energy, they can achieve extraordinary results – and sometimes in an unbelievably short amount of time.

I witnessed this when my children were at primary school. Each year the school's Parent–Teacher Association would rehearse and stage a pantomime in just three weeks. The purpose? To raise thousands of pounds for the school.

It would be an amazing three weeks, watching the combined force of teachers, children and parents come together every evening – and all day at weekends – to transform a simple school hall into a little theatrical haven. I once walked in to see a dance rehearsal for the dads. The troupe comprised an optician, an architect, a landscape gardener, an accountant and the landlord of the local pub – some still in shirt and tie, having come straight from work, but sporting part of their costume – green tights – so they could 'move more easily' onstage.

Rehearsals usually began at 7 p.m., but often the hall would already be buzzing by 6 p.m. – a creative powerhouse. Set painting, costume fitting, music rehearsals, light rigging and, of course, child corralling. One evening, I overheard one dad say to his dance partner, between *pliés*, 'Do you know, I can't remember the last time I managed to get home before 7 p.m. and here I am in my green tights by 6.30.'

Over the best part of a decade, this injection of a collective purpose energy resulted in hordes of thrilled audiences, thrilled performers, a thrilled bursar and finally the thrill of an unsuccessful tax investigation by HMRC who could not believe a state primary school could raise so much money solely through the efforts of a mere PTA.

The experience gave everyone involved a real sense of fulfilment. As a consequence, parents who stepped forward once to make a small contribution would return year after year, often wanting to take on 'something bigger'.

Some people refer to this energy as spirit.

In 2005, Hurricane Katrina devastated New Orleans. When the hurricane hit, a shipyard in the city had been in the middle of constructing a new ship, the USS *New York* – which has a compelling story attached to it. In the aftermath of the storm, thousands of workers were drawn back to work on this ship, despite many of them losing their homes to Katrina. Some began living at the shipyard. Others even postponed their retirement. The head of the shipyard, Philip Teel, described their dedication and devotion to duty as 'epic'. Why such a strong sense of purpose? The 7.4 tons of steel used to create the USS *New York*'s bow had been salvaged from the 9/11 World Trade Center disaster. When the steel was being melted down, a navy captain said, 'The big rough steelworkers treated it with total reverence. It was a spiritual moment for everybody.' The manager of the foundry added, 'It had a big meaning for all of us.' The ship's motto was 'Never Forget'.

The essence of connecting to the power of purpose beyond self-interest is beautifully summed up by Teel. 'It sounds trite, but I saw it in their eyes. The fact that the ship has steel from the Trade Center is a source of great pride. They view it as something incredibly special. They're building it for the nation.'

This example was, of course, an extraordinary reaction to

an extraordinary moment in time. Charities are groups of people who are bonded together by this kind of purpose beyond self-interest, and who demonstrate it on a daily basis.

A particular favourite of mine is a wonderful drama project in London called Scene & Heard. They work to build self-esteem, confidence and creativity in children (starting aged nine or ten) from the area around an infamous council estate in north London. The selected children are encouraged, through workshops over several months, to create small plays which are then produced in a theatre in London by theatre professionals – directors, actors, costume designers, prop-makers, stage managers – all of whom do the work totally free of charge. And when I'm in the audience and see the child playwrights' beaming smiles as they receive the applause and acknowledgement, I completely understand why.

The Delancey Street Foundation in the United States is another example. A hugely successful rehabilitation programme, it was started in the 1970s and co-founded by Dr Mimi Silbert, a criminologist who contributed her own salary to the purpose of the foundation: to help drug abusers, ex-convicts and the homeless turn their lives around. She instilled the key principle of 'Each One Teach One' in the residents – focusing on their strengths. There is an expectation that each resident is responsible for helping introduce and guide the new arrivals. So, over time, her purpose became their purpose – demonstrating her belief that the people who are seen as the problem can, themselves, become the solution. It now has an annual budget of about $18 million and houses and educates some

2,000 people at any given time across the country – all thanks to the force of a purpose beyond self-interest.

Purpose beyond self is an energy that we can all connect to. It's unleashed when we tap into our deepest values and connect to something worthwhile and meaningful for others. When we do this it can invigorate all our other energies. When something really matters to us, it provides a powerful source of motivation, focus and determination. It can help us keep going even when things are out of our control.

Victor Frankl survived a Second World War concentration camp through connecting to purpose. He imagined himself in the future – after his release – giving lectures. Specifically, he envisaged helping others understand what the concentration camps did to people. By doing this, he managed to lift himself out of this immediate suffering. He wrote: 'We must never forget that we may also find meaning in life even when confronted with a hopeless situation, when facing a fate that cannot be changed.'

There is certainly a force to be drawn from purpose energy. I observe it in stories like Frankl's, and witness it in the people I work with when they connect to it. The question is, how can we connect to the power of it when we need it? It can all too easily be eclipsed by the drive to strive, to keep doing the doing, to get on with the daily tasks. How could you more intentionally connect to purpose energy? To fire up the force?

In my clients' desire to be better, the questions that most help them connect to this extra force are: why does it matter to you, and who else will benefit? Sometimes they have to just *keep* asking those questions in order to shift from focusing on a goal to a bigger purpose. I learnt that, to be the most useful teacher to the young people in my care, it was essential I understood what mattered to them. When I asked students why school mattered, they usually replied with answers like 'getting a job', 'going to university', 'dunno'. However, with further thought, they would often end up giving answers involving others: 'I want to make my mum/ my dad/my family proud.' Then I saw the energy shift.

When people connect to the power of purpose, I witness them move from:

- invisible to invigorated
- indecisive to incisive
- older to bolder
- strung out to strong
- confused to confident
- giving up to giving everything

> I know that every time I felt a class was becoming more of a challenge or a student was becoming less motivated it was always worth leaning in further and asking, 'What matters to you?' How can coming to school help you achieve that? How can connecting to that help?' Whenever I did that – however difficult

the conversation – I would witness them push forward. They might persist with a piece of homework, or turn up to that next rehearsal, or generally engage more. It always reconnected me to why I wanted to be a teacher too. It fired me forward. I began to learn that connecting them to a bigger purpose fuelled both an energy in them *and* in me. I saw it as a vital component to learning, and started deliberately paying more attention to it and creating space for 'purpose' conversations in lessons.

There are several levels to purpose. The most powerful is when your *why* is clearly attached to a cause that is much more than simply satisfying your personal needs or goals.

How well do you connect yourself, your family, the people you lead, or your customers, to purpose energy?

Here are some questions to help power it up:

- What really matters to you?
- When have you felt the power of purpose energy?
- How would you describe yourself when you connect to it?
- What makes you come alive?
- Who inspires you to be better?

- Who in your life has it? How do you recognize it?

- In ten years' time, what will be important to you?

- What would you like to overhear someone saying about you if you were to fast-forward five years? Ten years? Twenty years?

- How do you want people to remember you?

- What do you want to contribute to the world?

And here are some top tips to help you connect to it:

- Connect what you're doing now to who will benefit.

- Connect to it every day: create a purpose energy practice, including a 'meaning for others' mantra and/or a purpose trigger.

- Connect any tricky task to a 'higher' purpose.

- Make time regularly to see or speak to the person/group who inspires you.

- Choose an energizing purpose label to describe what you do.

- Write a letter to yourself from the future describing how you've made a positive impact on others.

Our Five Energies

Body Energy

Mood Energy

Mind Energy

Purpose Energy

People Energy

9.

CHOOSE TO CONNECT

'One of the things that we never discuss – or we rarely discuss – is the value and importance of human connection . . .'

Educator Rita Pierson

And finally, the fifth energy: people energy. This is the energy we receive from or give to others. The energy that comes with any interaction.

BOOST AND DRAIN

We all have people in our lives who energize us – just the very thought of them. We look forward to them attending a meeting or being at a social gathering because their energy makes us feel uplifted and positive. These are people who we might describe as motivating, optimistic, upbeat, appreciative, interested or thoughtful. People who boost us. One client described just such a booster by saying, 'As soon as I see her I smile. I feel reinvigorated. When I leave her, I feel I can achieve anything.'

At the same time, we also have people in our lives who have an unhelpful effect on our energy. They can make us feel exhausted, anxious or irritated. They are the ones who sit in meetings with disinterest or consistently point out what's wrong; perhaps they are 'needy' friends who rarely ask how you are, or a sibling who's always moaning. Their impact might be described like this: 'I only have to see them walking towards me and my heart sinks.'

We give off and pick up people energy signals all the time.

Let's revisit the three brains for a moment.

When we interact, all three brains are involved. At the

most primitive level, way before any words are spoken, humans sniff each other out to sense quickly, often subconsciously, whether others are food, a foe, a friend or a f**k, developing hunches about each other's real motives and intentions. Remember, our animal brains are programmed to assume anyone new is a potential threat until convinced otherwise. Boosters quickly help the Reptile and the Dog brains to assume 'friend'. The Reptile brain picks up the body signals: a smile; their eyes; the way they're standing or sitting. The Dog quickly interprets, 'The smile looks genuine, the eyes are warm, the body is open. Yes, all is good. Friend. It's safe.' If you've met this booster before, then your animal brains will recall the feelings they previously provoked and will predict the same outcome. They've created a positive story about this person and, as a consequence, will increase your energy for any future interaction with them.

Drainers, on the other hand, send the opposite type of signals. So, if someone has drained the hell out of you in the past, or made you feel stupid or angry, your energy for any future meeting with them *decreases* and an *un*helpful story emerges. Just as we run stories about ourselves that might help or hinder our ability to choose our mood, so we run stories about other people – what we believe about them and what we believe they think of us. Our story affects their story, which in turn then affects ours again . . . and so it continues. It's contagious. Our animal brains and their animal brains 'conversing' back and forth.

I remember when my son, Charlie, took his Grade 5 saxophone exam aged eleven. His exams up to this point had been taxing, but he had enjoyed the experience and passed them all. On this occasion we were sitting in the waiting room and through the wall we could hear each student as they went in, played their scales, played their piece and then left the room. At the appointed time, Charlie bounced up out of his seat, looped his saxophone around his neck and marched out of the door. Over the next ten minutes, I heard all the hard practice he had done in readiness for the exam go completely up in smoke. As I craned to hear, there were some uncharacteristically staccato scales and then a torturous rendition of 'Watermelon Man'. He just about managed to salvage it, came running out and fought to hold back the tears.

In the car, we discussed what had happened. It seems that this exam was not like any of his previous ones. In the others, each examiner had been welcoming, chatted to him, smiled at his responses and basically made him feel comfortable. This time, he walked in and, according to him, 'there was no smile'. The examiner was monosyllabic in his responses and 'there was no expression on his face – the whole time. I became so nervous.' The examiner was probably giving off a neutral 'professional' air, but my son's previous experiences had led his Reptile and Dog brains to expect a friend behind that door. This time, when he found himself opposite Mr Neutral, the Reptile and Dog sniffed a foe, pulling Charlie's focus away from playing the music as well as possible and instead pointing his attention to a likely threat. Rather than focusing his mind energy on playing the music as he had practised, they became involved in creating a story about a man who didn't like him and was out to see him fail.

We tune in to other people's signals and they tune into ours. We can make instant decisions about them and what they might think of us based on these signals – the power of the 'people energy airwaves'. On the whole, a 'booster' or a 'drainer' may have no idea they are having this impact on us. Similarly, we too could be having the very same impact and be blissfully unaware.

Most people energy is unintentional and sent out unconsciously – that's why it's an area deserving our care and attention. A key way to manage people energy is to choose the most useful positive stories about others. As with all energies, paying attention to it takes deliberate effort. Have you got an unhelpful 'story' you're running about someone – a story that is impacting your interactions and the people energy you give to and receive from them?

I once sat with a client who spent the first thirty minutes telling me how draining and irritating she found someone she was working with. 'When I think about having a meeting with him,' she told me, 'I think, '*Oh no, that irritating person who is going to talk too much and suck up my time.*' I wanted her to run a more useful story about him, so I asked her to focus on *one* thing she could appreciate about him. As with many clients when faced with this question, she found this difficult.

Eventually she replied, 'Well, he has recently completed a trek to Everest base camp for charity and was part of a party who offered to support someone back down who'd been injured.'

I said how impressive that was and she quickly added, 'He told me that in GREAT detail.' That last comment showed how easily the old story could slip back in. So I asked her to deliberately think of his Everest story whenever she saw him – *without* the last comment she'd tagged on. When we next met, she said, 'It's taken effort – and it's a lot harder to do if I'm tired – but I do admit that actively choosing to see him as "that person who carried someone down from Everest base camp" definitely makes a difference to how I greet him. No question. I feel more motivated to make an effort and I've noticed he looks less intimidated.'

Our people energy can become a useful part of the way we interact, build relationships and even influence others. The way we listen to each other, for example, impacts people energy and has the capacity to boost or drain, increasing or limiting our ability to bring the best of ourselves to any task. I often see this in meetings I observe. Someone is talking and others are giving off signals, either consciously or not.

Common Boosting Signals	Common Draining Signals
Being alert and present	Looking at your phone
Nodding	Thinking about something else
Smiling	Giving others a wry smile

Showing genuine interest	Looking frustrated or bored
Active listening	Interrupting
Asking curious questions	Contributing nothing

Either way, the impact on how the other person feels can be significant. I know that when I sense that someone isn't listening to me, it can very quickly spark an unhelpful story in my head: 'They clearly don't think I'm very interesting or worthy of their attention.' If I'm not careful, this in turn can cause me to do one of two things: talk faster and faster; or suddenly lose any grasp of the English language and fail to articulate what, only moments ago, was very clear to me.

Rather than leaving it to chance, it helps if the impact we're having is the one we want to have. A question I often ask a client is: 'Are you prepared to be 100 per cent accountable for your impact on others?'

People who are brave enough to say 'yes' are aware of and deliberately pay attention to how their energy, their words, their tone and their actions can affect those around them. Particularly in times of pressure. If you choose not to, it's high risk, because how you *feel* about someone can have more of an impact on them than what you say.

When we see one thing and hear another, we are more likely to believe what we see. The impact our energy can have on others' energy, confidence and productivity can be huge. So . . .

Thanks to Facebook, I am regularly put back in touch with former pupils. What they have to say can be eye-opening. One ex-student recently wrote:

> I really hope you are happy and I am happy to have made contact with you after all these years. I did enjoy your lessons but I always wanted you to ask me my opinion in class and you never did. I was one of the quieter ones. You had others you preferred to ask.

Another wrote:

> So glad to find you. I want to say thank you for two things: taking me to the dining hall when I had just arrived from my home country and couldn't speak English. You sat me at a table of people and I am still good friends with one of them. Secondly, whenever I used to say 'I can't do that', you would always say 'What if you could?' I still say that to myself and my children.

Sadly, I can't remember any of those things happening, but they clearly did and, what's more, these comments show that the moments have remained with those pupils right through into their adult lives. Now their comments remain with me.

We have such an impact without knowing it – as a teacher, as a parent, as a leader. The things we say to people – often in passing – can remain as stories and soundtracks deep in their being for years afterwards. How many people do you know who remember a teacher for the impact they had, good or bad? It can be something they leaked, let slip and thought nothing of that lives on into adulthood. I know my lack of confidence even now in Maths can be tracked right back to Mr Tubbs, looming over my shoulder during Maths O-level class. His sighs of frustration as I tried to fathom how much water was in the bath after Peter had pulled the plug out for five seconds before John got into it – probably standing on one leg while eating a crumpet or some other ridiculous situation that I felt bore no relevance to my life – still echo around my head when I'm looking at my accounts.

One of my clients, David, a successful senior partner in a high-profile law firm, regularly suffered from bouts of self-doubt, especially when he was offering advice to demanding clients. He wanted to find ways to boost his confidence in this type of pressured moment. In one session, we were planning an approach to one particularly challenging client when David randomly mentioned his old headmaster who used to give him 'a raised eyebrow of doubt'. I asked him what on earth he meant. 'Oh, I've never forgotten him raising that eyebrow when I mentioned that I wanted to try for Cambridge University.'

Now, the headmaster is not here to defend himself and his gesture may well have been one of delighted surprise, pride or even self-satisfaction, but the schoolboy David read this little leak as doubt. Now, some thirty years later, the successful lawyer David is still haunted by doubt thanks to that raised eyebrow.

What followed was a realization by David that this gesture had been gnawing away inside him for far too long and he had to do something with it. His reaction to it was draining his energy – energy he wanted to conserve for the clients he enjoyed working with and for his family.

That headmaster had no idea that what may have been only an involuntary tic would cause such a long-lasting chain reaction. Similarly, I had no idea that failing to ask a student for their opinion would sit with them for so long. A throwaway comment, an unintentional gesture – or lack of one – can all have an impact. And not only in education.

An executive wanted to give his undivided attention to anyone who entered his office, so he made a point of closing his laptop whenever they came in. It was only by chance that he discovered the staff were unsettled by this. It transpired that they read the closing of his laptop as him hiding stuff from them.

I was in an office foyer waiting for the lift to arrive and take me up to a client. When the doors opened, I entered with four other people, who were all having a relaxed chat. At the last moment, I heard very loud, fast steps approach the closing doors. In bustled a woman clutching a pile of documents with a very tense

> face. Her anxiety and stress was palpable. We
> all felt it and froze. For the remaining eight
> floors, all conversation stopped.

You probably know someone who, when you talk to them, makes it very evident when your time is up. They avert their eyes and that's your signal to move on.

A client recently described a meeting where a challenging suggestion was made by one of her colleagues. She was clearly leaking something when the colleague made his suggestion because he looked at her and said, 'Don't give me that face.'

And here's a fascinating, high-profile example of unconscious leakage from the world of rugby union. Sir Clive Woodward often linked up with the Royal Marines when he was in charge of the England team, and based many of his innovations on methods employed by them. Woodward credits the Marines with teaching him one vital principle. Prior to the 1999 World Cup, Woodward had been selecting players on match-playing abilities and skills. He put this squad through a gruelling four-day preparation exercise with the Marines and, afterwards, he asked the sergeant major for an honest appraisal of the players. According to Woodward, the sergeant major's response went something like this:

> I don't know if these guys are good rugby players or not.
> I don't know if they have superior skills to the others or

if they make better decisions under pressure than some that you've left behind. But I have to tell you, you've picked three men who we would not go to war with. In the Marines, we know there are certain people in life who live for themselves and only themselves. They are more interested in their own good, not the success of the team. If something goes wrong, it is someone else's fault. If they see themselves in competition with a colleague, they will undermine that person by making snide comments behind their back or lobbying others against them. They are not capable of taking personal responsibility for their own actions. They suck attention from those around them and don't give anything back. We call them energy-sappers.

Sadly for Sir Clive, it was too late to change the squad before the World Cup and England were knocked out in the quarter-finals. When the team reconvened, in Woodward's words, 'The sappers were all sorted out. Some I managed to turn around.' Most importantly, as he continues, 'In every case, none actually realized their impact on the team.'

In the squad for the next World Cup in 2003, there was 'not an energy-sapper in sight'. England won the World Cup.

The same is true in any team. Be it sport, the arts, corporations, friendships or families. So, watch what you leak.

Instead . . .

Why is it that teams tend to win more when they play at home? What do they mean by 'home advantage'? Apart from the fact that everything is more familiar – which helps to conserve their energy for playing the match – there is one other notable characteristic: very obvious home support. With the positive intent to boost, that home support does three things:

1. Tells the team the crowd is behind them and wants them to win.

2. Cheers good performance: 'Great pass!'

3. Offers improvement suggestions (though not always in the politest language!)

Cheering what is working and *then* offering a way of making it *even* better is the most useful way to help others improve. People can receive criticism like a personal attack on their status or their competence – which, to the brain, is perceived as a physical attack. People pain – the feeling of being put down, ignored or treated unfairly – used to be seen as something we just had to 'get over'. But neuroscience research by Naomi Eisenberger has now shown that the brain treats people pain much like physical pain. One study actually showed that Tylenol, a standard painkiller, reduced people pain more than a placebo. Similarly, people rewards are often treated like physical rewards in our brains. Telling someone what you like about them, thanking them, or appreciating what they have done well, can give them the same or even more hormonal reward than any financial remuneration.

Attacks are usually met with some kind of defensive strategy – the positive intent of our Reptile and Dog brains to protect us. This explains the significant number of conflicts, misunderstandings and tensions in our everyday life. Practising home support – the power of home advantage – in our conversations and meetings is a way of increasing people energy and often, as a result, confidence and belief in what is possible.

Feeling supported and appreciated has a positive impact on all of us. The skill is showing it in the way that is most useful.

We all know people who boost our energy. The late Rita Pierson, quoted at the start of this chapter, was an American educator for forty years who believed passionately that every child deserves a champion, 'an adult who will never give up on them, who understands the power of connection, who insists that they become the best they can possibly be'. To give you a sense of how she boosted others, here is a story she tells about a conversation she had with a student when she conducted a twenty-question quiz and, despite a student getting eighteen questions wrong, she put a '+2' on his paper with a big smiley face. This is how she recounts the story:

'Ms Pierson, is this an F?'
'Yes.'
'Then why'd you put a smiley face?'
'Because you're on a roll. You got two right. You didn't miss them all and when we review this, won't you do better?'
'Yes, Ms Pierson, I *can* do better.'

She finishes by saying, 'You see, Minus 18 sucks all the life out of you. Plus 2 says, "I ain't all bad."'

By deliberately focusing this pupil's attention on what he had achieved, Rita was lessening the influence of his Dog brain. She deliberately disrupted his primeval tendency to focus on what wasn't working by believing in him, appreciating him and boosting his confidence to persevere. The best people energy comes through appreciation.

We are more able to perform when we feel supported and appreciated too. When someone gives you more reason to believe, it powers up your mood energy. That is why it works. I've witnessed many examples of people or students who underperform in one team or class, get moved into another team or class and consequently flourish. When asked about the difference, they usually say they feel 'more supported', 'more challenged', 'more significant'. They have been seen in a 'new, fresh way'. The new leader or teacher is often running a more useful 'story'.

People energy can either improve or undermine the performance of others.

Liverpool were playing Sunderland at home in a Premier League football match in 2016. After seventy-six minutes the score was 2–0 to Liverpool and they were looking very comfortable. In the seventy-seventh minute, thousands of Liverpool fans had agreed they would leave the stadium in protest at the club's proposed ticket price increase. Despite the excitement of supporting a winning team, true to their word they left the stadium, leaving thousands of empty seats. Over the next thirteen minutes Sunderland scored twice and the game ended in a draw. A perfect example of what can happen when the home support is withdrawn.

I mentioned earlier how Professor Samuele Marcora's research revealed that cyclists improved their performance by 17 per cent when they heard subliminal words like *go* and *lively*. Well, his team also found that when these cyclists saw subliminal messages of happy faces they rode, on average, 13 per cent longer than those shown unhappy faces.

> Smiles boosting miles – a universal example
> of the power of home support on
> performance. People energy beyond words.

Who is your home support? How much time do you spend with them? Do you actively seek them out? Do others actively seek you? How can we be more deliberate about connecting with each other, to give and receive useful people energy?

When we're busy, it's easy to avoid making connections with others. It's often easier to concentrate on the transactional and task-driven nature of our interactions. I'm talking about emails too. I'm afraid I struggle with emails that are purely transactional. I know they make sense and save time when we are all so busy; however, I also know how a moment of human connection – even in three words – can make me feel more energized and motivated to respond. I am intentionally using the word *feel* because people energy is about feeling.

Like exercise, the more human connect moments you can sow, the more benefits you can grow. The benefits are accumulative. In other words, actively engaging in human moments on a regular basis can have an underestimated impact on you. For some people, deliberately setting up these opportunities is part of their daily routine. I have one client – a creative designer – who makes a point of meeting a creative person for coffee three times a week. The stimulating conversation is part of boosting his own creativity for the rest of the day.

By starting an interaction with a moment of human connection – it can be as short as twenty seconds or as long as five minutes – you give yourself an opportunity (and a choice) to connect to them as a positive person, even if you know you have different views or outlooks. The positive impact of a human connect moment can last long after the people involved have walked away. In organizations I witness people connect and start to think in new and creative ways together – people who have worked in the same organization for years, often in the same team, but who find out something new in that moment. Something that helps them connect 'human to human' rather than head of operations to head of finance, sales manager to customer, or even father to son. It is often a way of inviting some genuine honesty into the room.

Not long ago, a client of mine had been having a particularly tricky time working with one of her colleagues. This colleague had a reputation for being very abrupt, cold and confrontational. Recently, however, that colleague's father had died, a personal situation my client had also recently experienced.

A meeting was in the diary to continue a long-running discussion on an issue that they had failed to get to the bottom of. According to my client, when they met it was normally tense and difficult, each vehemently protecting their own area of the business.

This time it was different. My client chose to step into the human moment and shared her experience of recently losing her father; the other followed. The relationship shifted and so did the long-standing issue.

It may seem vaguely counter-intuitive to start a business meeting by connecting on a personal level; however, that human connection is energizing, memorable and can open doors that were previously closed. It allowed these two colleagues to move forward as two humans connected by a similar situation.

Suppose you haven't got a similar situation to connect with? Find out more about them. Work at it. Get curious. It's worth the effort.

Much to my husband's disappointment I'm no football fan, but it was football that gave me first-hand experience of the power of human connection.

There was a time in my teaching career when Sunday evenings were miserable. Around 7 p.m. I'd get butterflies in my stomach, as Lesson One on Monday – a Year 9 Drama class – loomed. About a dozen boys would regularly derail the entire lesson. They had absolutely no intention of taking Drama GCSE, but they still turned up. They were avid West Ham fans and most of the lesson was spent trying to stop them dissecting West Ham's weekend performance. To make things worse, they rarely turned up on time. The better-behaved students would be waiting patiently in their chairs, while I'd spend ten minutes getting the others into the classroom and calming them down. Typically, once I had most of them sitting down and ready to listen, two more would burst in and disrupt proceedings, and I'd be back to square one. That lesson usually left me exhausted, and I had to delve deep for any confidence that I could teach at all, let alone face the Year 7 kids expectantly waiting outside for Lesson Two.

I'd been at a loss as to what to do. I'd tried planning the lesson differently, tried an unusual classroom layout, even threats. I'd also taken advice – mostly from more senior staff, who'd say, 'Just send them to me.' The students saw me as the teacher, not as a human being, and didn't think I was on their side. I had to change things or the remaining eight months of our classroom time together would be hell for all of us.

One Saturday afternoon at around five o'clock, my boyfriend (now husband) became decidedly grumpy. We were meeting friends that evening and this mood would not be helpful. I asked what had happened. It transpired that his team, Liverpool, had lost to West Ham. Apparently he was angry with himself for even hoping Liverpool might win, as the Hammers were pretty much their 'bogey team'. I laughed – well, it was a ridiculous turn of phrase – and he went to great pains to explain what it meant and showed me how poorly Liverpool had fared against West Ham in the previous few seasons. I tried to sympathize, but all I could picture was those boys wrecking my first lesson of the week.

On Monday morning the class filled quickly, dominated by overjoyed, fidgety Hammers fans. Armed with my new-found knowledge, I took a deep breath and started a conversation with them.

'So, a weekend of celebration then?'

After a momentary look of disbelief that I would even dare to enter into a conversation with them about their weekend activities, one of them casually said, 'West Ham won again, miss.'

I continued with a smile. 'Yeah, but against Liverpool? Come on. The Hammers are pretty much their bogey team, aren't they?'

The effect was immediate. At first, they were totally thrown. They looked at me with a mixture of astonishment and amusement. You could see them weighing me up. They then called their mates over and gleefully reported my comment. Luckily, they agreed I was right and began to include me in their rendition of the game. Needless to say, I didn't understand much of what they said, but I listened and acted as if I did – because I hoped the longer gain would be worth it. Something was beginning to shift. This time it was easier for me to get their attention, lightly change the subject and draw them into the start of the class activity. This human-to-human interaction created a connection and therefore a different way forward. They felt as if I saw them as more than just disruptive time-wasters, and began to see me as possibly more than just a controlling, pain-in-the-arse teacher.

Thereafter, every weekend of the football season I made a deliberate choice to note West Ham's result and to form some opinion on the way they had played. Coached at home, I learnt a bit about the game. Come Monday, instead of sitting inside, waiting for them to 'land' in the room in whatever way they chose, I consciously stood outside the class and welcomed them in with a comment about the match.

Over time, this connection increased their desire to listen and commit and made the following months much more bearable for all of us, transforming a stroppy teacher with a bunch of unruly boys into a group of humans making the most of the next six months together. Or at least until the football season ended.

Sometimes, the more you know about someone, the easier it is to develop an alliance. We can change our stories about others and in turn be changed ourselves.

DO — FEEL — KNOW

So, how about influencing through people energy? In the world of theatre, finding the answer to this question is a basic part of an actor's preparation, helping him or her to make their performance of a character as believable as possible, and creating a meaningful connection with the audience. A director once asked me, 'What are you doing to the other character with that line, Sara? What's your emotional purpose?'

Think about your emotional purpose or, as I call it, the *feel purpose*.

When I work with people who wish to become better at connecting and bringing the most useful people energy into an interaction where they want to influence others, I usually ask, 'What's the purpose of this meeting? Interaction? Conversation?' They might reply with any of the following:

- To let them know . . .
- To give them a sense of . . .
- To share information about . . .
- To update on . . .
- To tell them . . .
- To inform them . . .

These purposes all focus on passing on knowledge. These are all answers to the question 'What do you want them to know?' This is usually the only thing people focus on when they want to influence. And it might be enough. However, informing is different from influencing. Influencing is about understanding what you want the person to *do* with that knowledge after your interaction. Once you have a sense of that, you can then consider the question 'What do you want them to *feel*?' (The feel purpose.) When you know what you want the other person to *do* as a result of the interaction, that guides how you want them to *feel*. Then it is time to edit your content accordingly and choose what you want them to *know*.

When we begin to think about feel purpose in

interactions, it can usefully affect all our people-energy transmitters. For example, say I want to support a friend who's going for a job she's not sure she's capable of. I want her to apply for it with confidence (*do* purpose), so I spend a bit of time thinking about how I'd like her to feel. I want her to feel reassured (*feel* purpose). This enables me to define what I need her to know: her strengths (*know* purpose).

What helps me when I connect to the feeling of reassurance is that I myself then start to feel more re-assured too. It also begins to change the story I'm telling myself about her. That reassurance will be transmitted to her before I even open my mouth.

BE DELIBERATE ABOUT THE WAY YOU MANAGE YOUR PEOPLE ENERGY

As Emma Thompson said of the late Alan Rickman, he had 'the capacity to fell you with a look or lift you with a word'. Choosing the most positive thoughts and feelings you can maintain about people will mean you radiate the most useful people energy. It might take effort, but it can have a magical effect. To quote a client from a large pharmaceutical company recently, 'I can't quite believe I've finally got a meeting with this doctor after two years by starting with something as simple and obvious as a human connection point instead of PowerPoint!'

Top tips – much easier to do when your SHED is in order

- Choose the most appreciative story about the other person/people.

- 'Cheer' others when they do something that makes a positive difference.

- Ask for what you want rather than what you don't – and share why it matters to you.

- Ask yourself what you want them to *do, feel, know.*

Example 1 A mother who wants a more trusting relationship with her teenage daughter after increasing rows is preparing for a conversation with her daughter as a first step to rediscover a loving and trusting relationship. The current story the mother is running is: 'She's growing distant and is a stroppy teenager who thinks I'm too judgmental.'

What does she want her daughter to:

- **Do?** *Share with me the things that are on her mind so I can help her think them through.*

- **Feel?** *Acknowledged, reassured, surprised.*

- **Know?** *That I too have felt that I didn't know what to do and was scared and confused. Reveal a truth – share with her a true and relevant story from my past to help us connect.*

Example 2 A young, ambitious employee who wants more autonomy from her boss is preparing a conversation to agree some ways of working on an upcoming project. The story she is currently running is: 'He is so controlling and he clearly doesn't trust me to succeed if all he can do is watch over me the whole time.'

What does she want her boss to:

- **Do?** *Agree to let me run this project and agree times when I will update him.*

- **Feel?** *Impressed, convinced, motivated to support me.*

- **Know?** *The details of how I would approach the project and how I would include him, as well as examples of how I've successfully completed similar projects in the past.*

Example 3 A husband who wishes to reboot his marriage – the children have now left home – is preparing for a conversation with his wife. He wishes they could have a deeper meaningful connection as they grow older. The story he is running: 'We are slowly living separate lives – she might be having an affair. She thinks I'm too preoccupied with work and have little time for her now the children have gone.'

- **Do?** *Agree to spend a weekend away with me.*

- **Feel?** *Understood, loved, reassured.*

- **Know?** *How I feel, what's at stake, why that matters, how much I love her.*

Example 4 A colleague who is being regularly drained by the energy of a co-worker is preparing a conversation to find a way forward. The story he is running: 'All he does is moan – tells me how irritated he is by others and the way things are being run. I wish I could sit somewhere else.'

What does he want his co-worker to:

- **Do?** *Come to meetings with more energy and solutions.*
- **Feel?** *Positively challenged, surprised, motivated.*
- **Know?** *The impact he has on me and some clear things that would make a difference to my energy. What the team could then achieve together.*

Example 5 Separated parents want to establish routine and consistency for their children as they live separately. The ex-wife is preparing a conversation to have with her ex-husband in the hope of providing two different yet stable and safe environments in which their children can thrive. Current story she is running: 'He's angry and resentful as I am in a new relationship, which he thinks is damaging for the children.'

What does she want for him to:

- **Do?** *Agree to the suggestion of sharing two school days as well as alternate weekends.*
- **Feel?** *Supported, valued, motivated.*
- **Know?** *I have the children at the heart of this discussion, and I respect and hugely value him as their father.*

The Me Journey

10.

We all crave progress. While we hope to build a better future, just focusing on the present keeps us in the present. In order to focus more clearly on where we're heading, pressing Pause and reflecting on where we've come from – our past – helps us to gain a stronger understanding of who we are and what matters to us. This fires up a more vivid sense of our future – what we want to be better at and who we want to be.

We are all trying to do our best with competing priorities: 'Do I go for that promotion?', 'Should I leave?', 'Should I stay put?', 'Do I start a business?', 'Do I start a family?', 'Do I start a relationship with that person?', 'Do I walk out of this relationship?' And some of us are trying to do our best when we haven't been given a choice: finding ourselves redundant, out of a relationship, bereaved or unwell.

Any of these situations can leave us grappling for a clear way through – juggling our own hopes and ambitions with the needs of others and wanting to do everything to the best of our ability. In these circumstances, it's easy to be left feeling overwhelmed or simply 'stuck'.

In my experience, people make better choices and the most progress when they take the time to explore three questions:

1. Who am I?

2. Who do I want to be and why?

3. What will I try next?

In an article by Academy award-winning actress Lupita Nyong'o entitled 'Why I Chose a Small Play over the Big Screen', she explains why she chose to turn down lucrative Hollywood projects in favour of performing in a play on Broadway called *Eclipsed* about five Liberian women surviving civil war. She writes, 'What I am learning is that the most important questions you can ask yourself are "What do I want?" and "Who do I want to become?"'

Most clients come to me having spent a lot of energy trying to answer just the third question. It makes a real difference if you answer all three questions – and in this order. Lifting yourself out of fixating on the last question to focus on the others first will boost your motivation to act. Ultimately, it will help clarify your answer to what you will try next.

The first question, 'Who am I?', might prompt you to go on an existential exploration. Or to state your name, age and current situation. Actually, I'm asking you to simply look behind you. To pick out a few trophy moments to help you feel proud of who you are and what you've already achieved. Connecting the dots between where you've come from and where you are now is what will enable you to move forward. So open up your trophy cabinet and reconnect to your strengths, passions and values.

When I first met Mary she was feeling stuck. Yet everything about her was fast: her speech, her gestures, her general manner. She had a diary madly full of meetings, a schedule that seemed relentless and a very demanding boss. On top of this, she had spent the last few years as a single mother raising two boys after leaving an abusive marriage. While from the outside she appeared to be a successful, ambitious woman, she was increasingly unhappy at work and frustrated that she wasn't clear about what to do next. She knew she was papering over the cracks of dissatisfaction with busyness. 'I feel like I've only got one foot on the floor. Up to now, I've always recognized myself as someone very committed, resilient, driven, and all about outcome and progress.'

Now it seemed that all of those things had become opaque because she had lost sight of her sense of purpose – her destination.

'I don't know where I'm going. I feel ill-equipped to go anywhere. I have all this good stuff around me but don't feel able to go forward.'

I asked her what she meant by 'good stuff'. She replied that she had a senior role in an organization and more personal security as a consequence. Her kids now had jobs of their own too, meaning she had more freedom.

To focus Mary on Question One, I asked her to tell me a few stories about her proudest moments. She struggled. She seemed to be filtering. She'd begin and then stop, censoring herself.

As she talked, we both realized that there were three very different versions of Mary – representing different eras of her life – that were obscuring her clarity. I asked her to describe the three versions. She could create a very clear picture for one, but found the others much harder.

She realized she had cut them both out, feeling they were no longer useful to her. 'They're holding me back and aren't relevant to me now. In fact, I'm slightly embarrassed by them,' she said.

Mary found understanding that very helpful. I encouraged her to share one proud story from each of the three different Marys. I could see she was still struggling. I pushed: 'What would they say they were most proud of, if they were here in this room right now?'

This galvanized her, and she got up from the chair and moved to one area of the room. 'Work Mary is here,' she said, and related one of her proud stories. She then crossed to another area and said, 'Mum Mary is here, and this is what she would say . . .' Finally she moved to another area and labelled the third Mary 'the little one, trying to make sense of the other two'.

Not everyone has to move around the room to access their proud stories. Not everyone has different versions of themselves either. But for Mary, moving into those different spaces helped her connect with and articulate all three trophy moments. It acted as a springboard.

By hearing them I began to understand their individual strengths. They helped me survive a very challenging situation: stuck in an abusive marriage that I wish I'd left a lot sooner. I've always felt bad about that for my children, and perceived Mum Mary as weak and accepting. By listening to her, I now understand that she was doing her best to keep a family together for the boys. Work

Mary was providing the financial independence and confidence I needed to leave. The little one was understandably scared and feeling lonely. I can now recognize and give a cheer to all three versions of Me as a past I'm proud of rather than ashamed of.

Having this opportunity to reframe, Mary began to see that she'd actually managed to keep a family together while also holding down a great job. I asked her to update her trophy cabinet.

I'd locked a few memories away but in a different cabinet altogether. Like the time my husband drove to my work, burst into the boardroom and trashed me in front of all my colleagues. I'd stored that in my 'Horrific Professional Moments' cabinet. Now I've taken it out and reframed it. I think, despite all his abuse, I managed to land a board position and survive. I'm now beginning to believe my boys when they say, 'You've given me the confidence that I can do anything.'

Over the next few weeks Mary deliberately focused on the positives from her past so that she could believe, like her boys, that anything is possible. She created positive triggers to help her: encouraging Post-its on her mirror that she could see first thing in the morning; and a playlist with three songs that represented the courage and determination all three Marys had given her. 'I have tripled my energy to think about where I want to go and have a much more stable platform from which to do it,' she told me.

Once you are clear and confident about where you have come from you can put your mind to where you want to be. Or, as one client put it, 'Picking up all of me from my past, making it proud, and striding with him into the future.'

As the saying goes, energy flows where attention goes. Focusing on what is going on in the present often keeps us where we are. This might be fine. You might be content with the present. However, if you are after a better present, and want to make better choices, it helps to connect to your even better future. The next step is to focus on Question Two and ask yourself, 'Who do I want to be and why?'

The aim here is to take yourself out of the present, buoyed with the confidence from your trophy cabinet, into the future you want.

Interestingly, if I ask a 'stuck' client what they want, they often launch into what they don't want: 'Well, I know I don't want to still be feeling like this in a year' or 'I don't want to be around X any more' or 'I'm sick of being told what I need to do all the time.' I watch them as they paint a very clear 'Don't Want' picture – a well-rehearsed scenario of what they want to move away from rather than what they want to move towards. *Physically* moving into your future can help you. I once witnessed sixty leaders of a global organization confidently stride from one side of a large room (their proud past) across to the far wall (their proud future). When I first met them they were a disparate bunch of senior individuals gearing up for a challenging

few months ahead and preoccupied with their own concerns and needs. Here, striding across the room, was an
emboldened group heading for a future they wanted to
create. It might have looked slightly ridiculous to any passing hotel staff, but literally moving into the future gave
these leaders clarity and courage.

Make your picture of your future as compelling and vivid
as possible. Focus on:

- Making it as sensory as you can – feel it, see it,
  hear it.

- Moving forward. Define a future space and move
  into it – literally.

- Describing it as though it has already happened.
  What have you done?

Talking about that future in the present tense actually fools
our Dog and Reptile brains. Because we're talking as if we've
already achieved the future, the Dog and Reptile relax. After
all, there's no likelihood of imminent threat when it's already
been achieved. And when we relax, we take the pressure off
ourselves in the present and open up possibilities. This kind
of imagining has been used in sport to great effect. When
Chelsea got relegated in 1962, manager Tommy Doherty
made sure that by Easter 1963 they were odds-on to bounce
straight back up into the top division. However, things
slipped and they started losing matches. They had only four
matches left when Doherty took the team out to dinner. He
told them to celebrate. He spoke to them as if they had been

promoted – even reminding them how they did it. They won the league and were indeed promoted.

I wanted Mary to be confident and imagine herself in a clear, positive, bold future. I asked her to walk across the room into her future and describe it – to firm it up in her present. This is what she said:

> I am running my own successful business with someone else. I am using the best of my experience and the product is making a difference to people's health and well-being. I'm involving experts. I left my old job decently – in a manner I was proud of. I'm really happy working for myself. It's challenging in a positive way. I have more freedom and choice. I have a team of people and we're all playing to our strengths. My new man and I have a wonderful place in Spain that we've spent the last five years doing up. It's a place we can both work from and gives us flexibility.

I watched Mary become more and more confident as she created the picture of her better future. I added further questions and she added more detail. I heard and watched her become stronger as she did so.

Later she told me, 'Standing in the future helped me experience it more fully. Speaking as if it had already happened makes it now feel easier, lighter.'

Joining the dots from your past betters to your future betters – bypassing any present blockage – creates the clarity and energy to answer the third question: 'What will I try next?'

So how did Mary answer this? What was that first step towards her new future?

'My first step towards my ambition is to remain confident and strong for the next six months in my current job while I plan my start-up,' she told me.

Once Mary had established her first step towards the future she envisaged, we agreed on a few more practices that would support her and build on the ones she was already finding useful:

- **Practice 1:** Reading a Post-it note on my dressing-room mirror that says: *Everything else has changed and work will too.*

- **Practice 2:** Asking 'What do I want to wear today?' By putting forward my best self, I am managing my image to set me up for success. I will always make sure I factor in enough time to do that.

- **Practice 3:** Listening to a playlist on the way to work. The work I'm currently doing is demotivating and I need to up my energy by connecting to the bigger ambition and why each day matters.

- **Practice 4:** Wearing a ring with three stones. The ring is me and the three roles I've played throughout my life to bring me to where I am today. I am now joined up and feel whole. Before I had only one foot on the floor. Well, now it's my floor and I'm building it – so I can stay stable.

So, what happened?

Mary left her senior corporate role and set up her own business, drawing together a team of high-profile experts. She has since secured the financial commitment of international investors and her business has already embarked upon delivering its first services. She's achieved all this in less than one year since first describing her better future.

Of course, not all of her journey went to plan. You may recall that her future story included setting up a business with someone else. And she did – with Claire, an expert in the field. However, six months later, tragically, Claire was diagnosed with cancer and died soon afterwards, leaving behind a husband and three young children. Mathematically, the power behind setting up Mary's business was now halved. However, with Claire's 50 per cent of the business signed across to a trust for her children, Mary holds their future in her mind and her purpose has been strengthened even further. 'This journey continues to stretch and test both my resilience and focus,' she told me, 'but deliberately paying attention to the practices ensures that both personal and commercial success feel within reach.'

Mary came to me as a successful leader who was stuck – unable to choose the most useful next step towards a more fulfilling future. Together we worked out a way to help her move forward. She discovered that she was better equipped to make progress by appreciating her past rather than being embarrassed by it.

Here are some questions you might want to ask yourself to help join your dots.

Who am I?

To become clear and confident about where you've come from, ask yourself:

- When am I at my happiest, most confident and fulfilled?

- What stories might I tell about when I've been at my best?

- What do these stories tell me about my distinctive areas of strength?

- What are the conditions that enable me to be successful?

Who do I want to be and why?

To become clear and positive about the direction you want to travel in, ask:

- What stories might I tell about the person I want to be?

- What do I want to be known for?

- What have I achieved in this future?

- How do I want to describe myself in this future?

- Now try answering these again as if that future has already happened.

What will I try next?

To make the next part of the journey as purposeful and as much fun as possible, ask:

- What would my first step be towards my vision of myself in the future?

- What will I choose to be better at?

- Given the way I learn best, what is my plan?

- What does my future vision reveal about what I need to stop doing?

Troubleshooting

11.

Making better choices is easier when you:

1. Fuel your Reptile brain to provide enough BODY energy.

2. Calm your Dog brain to provide the most useful MOOD energy.

3. Apply practices and techniques to focus and sustain your MIND energy.

4. Connect to something that matters to you and boost your PURPOSE energy.

5. Create positive PEOPLE energy with those around you.

If you were sitting in front of me with a situation you wanted help with, I would ask you specific questions — questions that would vary depending on your answers — to gain a sense of you and your circumstances. Together we

339

would look at possible ways forward based on your answers.

I don't have that privilege with you. So below I have listed a few situations that people often want help with. In each case I have listed a few tips that have moved people forward in moments that matter and can help you too.

That moment when . . .

You keep losing it . . . and wishing you hadn't.
It sounds like your Reptile and Dog brains are bossing you and your Human brain has relinquished control.

Tip 1: Look after your body energy. Which part of your SHED might give you more body energy so that you can have more choice over your mood?

Tip 2: Become aware of the first 'losing it' signals. What does your body do? Does your face go red? Do you become tense? Does your heartbeat race?

Tip 3: Interrupt the bossy brains and get yourself back to 'neutral' by focusing on your body posture and then your breath. Slow, calm exhalations.

Tip 4: Create a 'stay calm' mantra that you can use to reassure your bossy brains and give you choice.

Your friend is increasingly needy . . . and you find yourself avoiding them because they drain your energy.

You may want to prepare yourself before you see them. Try these:

Tip 1: Look after your SHED and arrange to meet when you feel well fuelled.

Tip 2: Create an appreciative self-talk in advance so you can have it at the ready if you need it.

Tip 3: Connect to a positive story about your friend before you meet, e.g. when have you had your best times together? What do you appreciate about them?

Tip 4: You might choose to make a request of them: 'I've noticed that we have our best times when . . . 'How about we . . . ?'

Your confidence takes a hit . . . and you find yourself shutting down.

This could be when you feel cut out of a conversation, disappointed by your own performance or judged. You need to recover it quickly. A few things you might want to try . . .

Tip 1: Choose a confident body posture. This could be something as small as lifting your gaze, smiling, pulling your shoulders back or choosing to stand up and move around.

Tip 2: Concentrate on your breath. Slowly exhale for a count of seven or focus your attention on slow, even breaths. You can do this without anyone knowing.

Tip 3: Connect to your strong positive trigger or self-talk. If you find this hard, make sure you develop one or two so they're right there when you need them. Find them from a time in the past when you felt confident.

Your boss is in a bad mood . . . and you have a scheduled meeting with him or her.

Your animal brains will be standing by for any likely 'attack'. Be deliberate about preparing yourself to keep your Human brain in control.

Tip 1: Before you go into the next meeting, choose your mood (rather than let *their* mood choose you).

Tip 2: Choose the most positive story about them so you are in a better position to bring positive people energy in with you as a boost.

Tip 3: Stay light and curious.

Tip 4: Looking after your SHED will increase your ability to choose and maintain this mood and keep your animal brains from responding unhelpfully.

Your child wants more confidence . . . to hold their own in class, in an interview, with a peer group or to try something new.

Help them develop some simple 'confidence practices' to prepare them for the next moment when they want to look, sound and feel more confident – practices to deliberately repeat *before*, and call on *during*, that moment. Encourage them to transfer those skills.

Tip 1: Ask when have they felt most confident. Encourage them to describe themselves in that confident moment. If they struggle, tell them when you see them at their most confident. Describe what you see in their body posture and hear in their tone.

Tip 2: Act as if. What was their body posture in that moment? Try it now.

Tip 3: Help them focus their attention on what they want to be (forward) rather than what they don't want to be (away from).

Tip 4: Help them create their 'confidence practice':

- Confident body posture
- Calm breathing
- A confidence trigger, e.g. music
- Positive self-talk mantra to connect them to that moment

And drill them in this practice.

You're returning to work after maternity leave . . . and you want to manage everything well:

Be impressive at work, be there for your family and see your friends.

Tip 1: Reflect on what you have achieved while on maternity leave. Why does returning to work matter to you?

Tip 2: Stand in the future. Imagine it's a year since you returned to work. Looking back over a very fulfilling year, what moments are you most proud of? Say them in the past tense.

Tip 3: Write down the 'returning to work' ingredients in those stories that really matter to you and identify one or two simple first steps to achieving them.

Tip 4: Create times to be 'properly selfish' so you can fuel yourself to be there for everyone else.

You're on your way home after a stressful day . . . and you want to arrive home to those you care about feeling positive and fully present.

Tip 1: Five minutes before arriving, stop to choose your mood.

Tip 2: Choose your 'arrival story', e.g. 'I'm about to reconnect with the most important person/people in my life.'

Tip 3: Choose the most useful story about each person so you can give them a positive greeting to help them feel great in all three of their brains!

You're at a crossroads . . . and feel confused about what to do next. You may have many options or just know that you want to move on from where you are.

Tip 1: Where from? Reflect on and pick out a few moments – periods in the past – when you felt fully connected to what mattered to you. These might be times when you were happy, proud or usefully challenged. Write them down. Notice and capture all the elements that stand out to you.

Tip 2: Where to? Move into a different place – a 'future' space. Choose to be five, ten or twenty years in the future. Have a play. Either write down or say out loud a few things you are doing in that future that make you feel proud, happy and positive. Speak them/write them as if they have already happened, e.g. Where were you? Who was there? What were you doing/causing? How did it make you feel? What did you see? What did you hear?

Tip 3: Write down your first step towards that future. What can you do immediately to move forward?

You want to succeed at that interview . . . and don't know how to start preparing for it.

- **Tip 1:** Connect to why getting this job matters to you.

- **Tip 2:** What do you already know about the people who are interviewing you? What else can you find out?

- **Tip 3:** As part of your preparation:

  - Do – What do you want them to *do* as a result of meeting you?

  - Feel – What do you want to make them *feel* during the interview?

  - Know – Based on all the above, what therefore do they need to *know*?

Over to You

12.

At the start of this journey, I mentioned how many of us increasingly want to achieve more in less time. And how we place pressure on ourselves to do all of it really well. None of us can be at our best all of the time. If you've been reading this and have already made a long To-Do list of the many things you want to be better at, please stop. Choose no more than two to focus on for the next month or so. Make yourself a drink of your choice and settle in an environment where you feel relaxed.

Now, think of the week or month ahead and choose maybe a couple of moments in that time that really matter to you. Moments where – if you paid them more attention – you could be even better. It might be an important meeting you're running; dinner with someone who makes a real difference in your life; a critical business decision you have to make. Moments that matter deserve your effort. Identify those moments in your 'better journey' and pay attention to them. Develop the habit of identifying them and release yourself from the pressure to do everything perfectly. Sometimes good enough really *is* enough. It's a vital choice we can make to conserve our energy so we have plenty for those moments that really matter in our lives.

I've shared the key players (three brains) and the supporting cast (five energies) with you. Now you can choose to manage them in the way that makes most sense for you. Everyone's way is different. It just has to work for you. Stay light and curious, focus on where it's working and, where possible, remember to laugh. The effort is eased when you can make it fun.

Recently I attended a performance by spoken-word artist Kate Tempest. She opened by asking everyone to turn off their devices so they could stay present, focus and, as she put it, 'be with me on the journey'. I ask you to do the same and be with you on your own journey.

I hope I have fuelled your curiosity enough to entice you to have a play with your choices as you venture on your voyage. I hope that, through this method, you find ways to make better choices and build really useful habits to keep flourishing and to become better – whatever *better* means to you.

And remember: wherever you hope to end up, it all starts in your SHED.

Acknowledgements

I was encouraged to write this book as an 'I' book when it is very much a 'we' book. The 'we' includes many wonderful people who I have had the privilege to learn from and work with. In particular the talented Coaching Impact team. The practices in the SHED Method have evolved and strengthened in collaboration with them and with the love and care of the CI home support team; Jennie Lanksford, Anna-Marie Wilby, Gemma Holden, Linda Royce and Jan Lewis.

I am also grateful to Jim Loehr & Tony Shwartrz, Paul MacLean, Anders Ericsson and Bill Rogers. Their work continues to inspire and sits at the heart of many principles shared in this book – as does the teaching and rigour of Nina Hubbard and David Bass in ballet and violin respectively.

I have others to thank. Simon Scott, who has had a huge influence on the ideas in this book. He, I know, would like to acknowledge the inspiring influence of his father who helped introduce science to British Rowing, and the ethos and Commando spirit of the Royal Marines Family.

Mark McGuinness for his 'on call' guidance and support and Simon Pearsall for his artistic skill, generosity and unique humour.

I appreciate hugely the time and insights shared by, among others, Dr Nicki Dawson, Lizzie Bentley Bowers, Steve Williams OBE, Caroline Hall, Anna McCormick, Tara Donovan, Alison Lucas, Genevieve Shore, Abi Griffiths, Rachel Joyce, Hope Claydon, Emma and Danny Kruger, Suzi Bergman, Virginia Eastman, Diane Samuels, Kim Guest, Debra Woods and Claire Price.

Andy Rubin for his support, openness, and for the opportunity to act and learn with him.

Tessa Morton for her chat in the car that opened my eyes to what else was possible.

The PRH team: Louise Moore for encouraging and prodding me to write it based on very little evidence that I could. Jill Taylor my editor, for her energy and confidence in me as a first-time author and her intriguing ability to push me further with a smile. My agent, Sheila Crowley, for her strength.

I owe a massive debt of gratitude to all the students, clients and coaches I have worked alongside and learnt so much from over the years.

And finally to my family. My daughter Matti and my son Charlie – for agreeing to have aspects of their lives shared in the book and for putting up with me as I wrote it. And Chris, my husband, who has encouraged and believed in this book – often more than me. He sat with me through my confusions and doubts – and made writing it possible whilst supporting everything else in our family life. Eternally grateful.

We are Coaching Impact.

We coach leaders, teams and organisations to achieve more, learn faster and live better.

We nudge, so our clients can choose, use and adapt useful practices, for better impact in their moments that matter.

Clients' stories are our inspiration. And it all starts in their SHED.

Impact. For Good.
www.coachingimpact.co.uk